D1616359

Mohonk and the Smileys

A National Historic Landmark
and the Family That Created It

Mohonk · Lake · Mountain · House.

ALBERT K. SMILEY, Proprietor

1888 {SEASON OPENS MAY 29TH. CLOSES ABOUT OCT. 15TH.} 1888

NEW PALTZ, ULSTER COUNTY, NEW YORK.

Etching from E.J. Whitney's 1888 illustrated *Guide Book to Mohonk Lake*.

Mohonk and the Smileys

A National Historic Landmark
and the Family That Created It

Larry E. Burgess

Director Emeritus, A.K. Smiley Public Library, Redlands, California.

BLACK·DOME

www.blackdomepress.com

Mohonk
Mountain House

www.mohonk.com

Mohonk® Mountain House
New Paltz, New York

New Edition 2019
Mohonk and the Smileys: A National Historic Landmark and the Family That Created It is
published in cooperation with Mohonk Mountain House by Black Dome Press Corp.,
PO Box 64, Catskill, NY 12414, blackdomepress.com.

Originally published in 1980 as *Mohonk: Its People and Spirit: A History of One Hundred Years
of Growth and Service*, it was corrected and updated in 1996, revised in 2009 and reissued with a
new foreword and final chapter, and entirely revised, updated, and expanded with this edition.

ISBN: 9781883789916 (paperback); 9781883789923 (cloth)

Library of Congress control number: 2018959582

Front cover: Photograph courtesy of Jim Smith Photography.
Back cover: *Lake, Summerhouse and Sky Top*, Nelson Augustus Moore, 1894.

Design: Ron Toelke, Toelke Associates, www.toelkeassociates.com

Printed in the United States of America.

10 9 8 7 6 5 4 3 2 1

Contents

Guest on Lake Shore Bridge, c. 1895.

In memory of Bert Smiley, 1944–2018

Quaere Momentum Circumspice

To seek their monument, look about.

GATE PATH

Etching from E.J. Whitney's 1888 illustrated *Guide Book to Mohonk Lake*.

Foreword to the 150th Anniversary Edition

As we approach 2019, this is a special time in Mohonk's history. Celebrating the 150th anniversary of the operation of Mohonk Mountain House as an independent entity under the stewardship of the Smiley family offers the opportunity to reflect upon the history of this remarkable enterprise.

The first history of Mohonk, entitled *The Story of Mohonk*, was written in 1911 by Frederick E. Partington. Three later editions of Partington's work followed, which eventually included black-and-white photographic images of the Mountain House, its lands, and activities. Following the advent of Mohonk's 100th anniversary in 1969, the Smileys invited Larry Burgess to research and write a more substantial history. As my father, A. Keith Smiley, noted in his introduction to Larry's first edition of this work: "Now that Mohonk's resort history covers well over a hundred years, it is agreed by the members of the Mohonk family that it is time for both an updating and a new perspective. We are indeed fortunate to have a good friend available to write a new history of Mohonk. Larry E. Burgess, a resident of Redlands, California, the winter home of Mohonk's founder Albert and his twin brother Alfred, has the rare combination of keen interest, thorough knowledge of Mohonk and its people, and the necessary perspective."

This new and extensively updated edition of Larry's work chronicles developments during the recent decades including the transition to the fifth generation of Smiley family leadership. It also explores in greater depth the behind-the-scenes stories of some of the unseen hands that have contributed to Mohonk's success in embracing changes that were necessary to ensure its continuing evolution and relevance in a rapidly changing world. This edition is enhanced and enlivened by a trove of archival images, many being displayed here for the first time, thanks to the tireless efforts of Pril Smiley, a fourth-generation board officer and director, and Nell Boucher, Mohonk's archivist. Finally, I wish to echo my father's sentiments that we are indeed fortunate to have a historian of Larry's caliber as a steadfast friend of Mohonk who was willing once again to mastermind this latest updated telling of Mohonk's story.

I hope that you will read this book with interest and enjoy the ongoing story of Mohonk Mountain House. Thank you for joining us on our journey as it continues to unfold. ❧

Bert Smiley
Mohonk Mountain House
July 2018

View from
Garden
Overlook, from
a glass slide,
c. 1905.

Prologue

Generations of dedicated leadership and commitment to the protection and enhancement of the environment.

The United Nation's Environment Programme Award, 1994

People need to be aware of the fact that Mohonk is more than a resort, or that its architecture is landmarked – it is also a center for very good science, and a place where the world can learn a great deal.

Dr. Noel Brown, Regional Director of the United Nations
Environment Programme in North America, July 6, 1994

Twenty-five years before the publication of this book, on July 6, 1994, Mohonk Mountain House Historian Larry Burgess had the honor of introducing Dr. Noel Brown, Regional Director of the United Nations Environment Programme in North America. Brown was there that day on the occasion of the celebration of Mohonk's 125th anniversary to present the United Nation's 1994 Environment Programme Award in recognition of the Smiley Family's 125 years of stewardship of the land within and surrounding their resort. Burgess noted in his introduction that Brown, "no stranger, and a long-time friend of Mohonk," had focused on encouraging young people to participate as responsible and responsive environmental citizens.

Dr. Brown began by observing that in one year (1995) the U.N. would observe its 50th anniversary, and that "This, too, will be an historic event. At fifty, the United Nations will become the longest surviving multilateral, multifunctional organization in history." Later in his comments, Brown added, "And that is why I am so pleased to be here this afternoon to join in this celebration, this 125th anniversary. Because, at 125 years old, Mohonk antedates the United Nations by some 75 years. I don't want to develop a complex," Brown joked, "but we are a bit of a junior partner compared to Mohonk."

Brown noted that the United Nations is "the second experiment of this kind. And it may not be the last. The first, if you recall, was the League of Nations, which lasted only twenty years when circumstances beyond its control [World War II] served it the mortal blow. Today, likewise, the United Nations is confronted with circumstances that it, too, may not be able to control and its survival is thus not assured and cannot be taken for granted. It is not written that the United Nations will survive. In the post–Cold War world where everyone had hoped that this would be an era of peace and human prosperity, we find ourselves confronted with crises of new orders of magnitude, pervasiveness and intensity. Ethno-linguistic nationalisms and fundamentalisms are sweeping the world—where brother fights brother and no quarter is given. … And so, as it approaches its 50th year, the United Nations finds itself tested as never before. And there is no guarantee that it will pass the test."

Brown went on to discuss the resilience of Mohonk in surviving those 125 years that witnessed "some of the most dramatic and most momentous changes in the entire sweep of human history. … Through it all, Mohonk has persisted. It has persisted in a vision of human future and a reaffirmation and commitment to what is best in us. Somehow, Mohonk has managed to keep faith with what is best in us. So, today, we at the United Nations are proud to find an enduring organization that has managed to share our vision of a world at peace with itself—just in its transactions, tolerant in its relations, and in harmony with nature."

Referring to the Lake Mohonk Conferences on International Arbitration that were held between 1895 and 1916 and were discontinued when America entered World War I, Brown stated: "Those of us who have followed the history of Mohonk cannot help but be impressed by its strong commitment to human solidarity and peace and its tremendous work to that end. When the agenda had as its priorities the issues of war and peace, Mohonk was there. Historians will tell you that the prelude to the Hague peace conferences of 1899 and 1907 were spawned at this site"

Dr. Brown further acknowledged Mohonk's landmark conferences in the 1880s and 1890s that sought solutions to the plight of American Indians and African Americans—"When human rights were the top of the agenda," Brown observed, "Mohonk was there." And then Brown addressed the issue of the day: "When environmental issues began to dominate the scene in the 1970s, Mohonk had a record that it could present to the world that might help us." Brown continued:

This morning I had an opportunity to participate in some reminiscences, and in particular the work of Mr. Dan Smiley, perhaps the greatest authority on the gypsy moth in the United States. And something struck me about this place: it retains its power of observation. In a world aswirl with explosive and accelerating global change, you need a fixed point if you are to establish proper measures. Mohonk has become a kind of baseline, whether you are studying the gypsy moth or hazardous chemicals, and so the environmental community has much to be grateful to Mohonk for keeping faith with the Earth. But it has also provided a framework for genuine dialogue and consultation.

I was a product of the 1970s, when confrontation was the order of the day. Mohonk provided an oasis of serenity where one could engage in a nonpoliticized dialogue with a view to finding solutions. And many solutions were found here. ... Now we find Mohonk, as it enters the 21st century, reaffirming that commitment to global and human environmental solidarity.

Boat landing,
c. 1890.

In a passage particularly relevant to today's global environmental challenges, Brown stated:

We at the U.N. have reason to look to Mohonk to help us as we move through this extraordinary period of change. Ladies and gentlemen, a few months ago we issued our latest findings on the state of the environment: the Environmental Data Survey 1994–95, which British journalists immediately dubbed the definitive Doomsday Book. Now, we at the U.N. try to shy away from alarmist rhetoric. Our work is to enlighten, not inflame. And yet the findings were of such magnitude that the world should take notice. We stated then that the climate is indeed changing; that sea level is rising; that mountain glaciers everywhere are in retreat, which show that the energy balance of the planet's surface is now changing; that the resource stocks of the planet are now showing very serious stress because of population expansion and expansion of the world economies;

On Sky Top
Path, c. 1890.

and that such renewable resources such as fresh water, soils, forests and sea fish are now showing very, very serious signs of stress.

That is why the world needs places like Mohonk, with its historical depth and the kind of commitment that it has demonstrated, and the good science that it practices. I think that people need to be aware of the fact that Mohonk is more than a resort, or that its architecture is landmarked—it is also a center for very good science, and a place where the world can learn a great deal. We at the United Nations are extremely pleased that this science center is available to us and is able to reinforce the work. For these reasons we are honoring this afternoon the Mohonk Mountain House and the Smiley family.

The cluster of summerhouses at the beach was known as Swiss Lake Village.

Mohonk is more than a set of traditions and some agreeable facilities in a magnificent setting—what we might call "the crown jewel of the Catskills"—it is also a family committed to what is best in us. I cannot think of any better tribute in this United Nations "year of the family" than to salute the First Family of the Environment and the tradition that they have provided us. So, as we move toward the 21st century, complex and challenging, we, too, would like to join those who wish that Mohonk will continue for the next twenty-five years doing what it has done for the last twenty-five years. For these reasons the U.N. would like to present at this time its 1994 Environment Programme Award.

Dr. Brown then read the inscription on the award: "The United Nations recognizes the Smiley Family and Mohonk Mountain House for generations of dedicated leadership and commitment to the protection and enhancement of the environment and for their

Lake view framed by the East Porte-Cochere.

inestimable contribution to the cause of peace, justice and sustainable human development; 6 July 1994."

Brown ended his remarks: "In conclusion, I would like to leave you with just one simple thought: Carry on, Mohonk! The best is on your side!"

Bert Smiley accepted the award on behalf of the Smiley family, together with the leadership medal that bears the same citation, by saying, "On behalf of my family and of Mohonk Mountain House it gives me great pleasure to accept these awards and all I can say is that in view of the paramount importance of environmental protection and environmental stewardship in today's world, and also its importance in Mohonk's history, I can really think of no greater honor." ∾

Approaching the Mountain House along Garden Road, early 1900s.

1

An Outing to Paltz Point

"But in spite of the burnt trees and dreary surroundings of the little tavern, the lake was there and the rocks and the cliffs and the making of a fine estate."

Albert K. Smiley, 1907

The story of Mohonk really begins in Maine, on a cold, snow-bound, and windy day in March of 1828. But for Daniel Smiley and his wife, Phebe, the Maine winter was the least of their concerns. During the evening of March 17, Phebe had given birth to identical twin boys. While Quaker Smiley did not celebrate St. Patrick's Day, the new additions to his family made March 17 something of a "Smiley day" for Daniel, his family, and friends in Kennebec County.

Daniel and Phebe Smiley had their two boys recorded in the Quaker Meeting in Vassalboro as Alfred Homans and Albert Keith Smiley. Ancestry provided the twin brothers with a Scotch-Irish inheritance from their father and English Puritan from their mother.

From their first days in school, the Smiley brothers' identical appearance confused teacher and friend alike. Even their mother had difficulty telling Alfred from Albert. Albert recalled that when "brother and I were born we were so much alike that our mother tied ribbons on either our arms or legs, I do not remember which, to identify us." Albert also recalled that he and Alfred always worked together, walked together, slept together, had measles, mumps, and whooping cough together. Nor had they a separate article of clothing or money between them until they were forced to divide their possessions when, at age twenty-seven, Alfred married Rachel Mott Swan. "In the morning," mused Albert in later years, "we jumped into the first suit of clothes that came our way, no matter who wore it the day before." All of their school study and reading was done from one set of books and was done simultaneously. The world of the youthful Smiley brothers was not one of "mine," but rather "ours."

The Smiley twins graduated from Oak Grove Seminary in 1845 and intended to enter Haverford College, a Quaker school thirteen miles from Philadelphia. Since Haverford was temporarily closed at that time, they both entered the senior class when the college reopened in 1848. The twins graduated in 1849. In the meantime, the college hired them as instructors.

Their home in Maine inculcated them with an appreciation for education, a respect for hard work, and an ability for making friendships and good companions. More importantly, Alfred's and Albert's parents had imbued them with a firm conviction and vibrant belief in the Quaker reverence for life. Upon leaving Vassalboro for Haverford, the Smileys brought to their college experience a profound appreciation for nature, a respect for the interrelationship between people and their environment, and

Albert Smiley, before he came to Mohonk as owner, c. 1860.

a recognition of the importance of beauty in daily life. They left Haverford trained with the tools of scholarship. They came to the world instilled with a sense of mission and stewardship; they came identical in resemblance, united in purpose. This background would later translate into a remarkable and unique business.

After a career in teaching, Albert and Alfred became co-principals of Friends School (now called Moses Brown School) in Providence, Rhode Island. Alfred later moved his family to a farm in Poughkeepsie, New York, which he purchased in order to provide a suitable environment for his wife and six children.

The farm venture was another joint enterprise that Alfred and Albert undertook, although Alfred planned to settle there permanently with his family. Albert owned a little more than half of the 115 acres, while Alfred owned the farmhouse, the barns, and the other outbuildings. "We expected to live there for the rest of our lives ... ," Albert later observed.

But time and circumstance have a way of altering the best-laid plans. When not busy with farming, Alfred delighted in taking his family on long walks and picnics in new places. He knew many interesting facts about nature, acquired over the years of study and teaching. Because of his interesting narratives, family and friends eagerly accompanied Smiley on his

Alfred and Albert Smiley, 1890s. This was the most popular image that identified "the Smiley twins." Alfred is seated and Albert is standing.

walks. As a result of one of Alfred's outings, the lives of all his family were never to be the same.

Having completed the summer's harvest in September of 1869, Alfred Smiley decided to set off on one of his outings. A friend, Jacob Haviland, suggested that West Point or a place called Paltz Point would both be interesting areas to visit. After drawing lots to see where they would go, Smiley, his wife Rachel, daughter Susan, son Edward, sisters Rebecca and Sarah, and friends the Havilands, Underhills, and Ferrises set out for Paltz Point. The party took a ferry from Poughkeepsie across the Hudson directly west to Highland, and then drove horses and surreys up the mountain to the foot of Paltz Point, not far from the town of New Paltz, a community started in the seventeenth century by French Huguenot families.

After driving up wooded hillsides and rounding a bend in the road, Alfred Smiley and his party were confronted with a stunning vista. Before them lay the imprisoned waters of a small lake, called Mohonk,* surrounded by rugged glaciated rock formations, partially covered by a heavy growth of trees and shrubs. The views proved to be uninterrupted verdure. Huckleberry harvesters, following Native American tradition, had set fire to some of the ridges to increase yields. Alfred and the hardier members of the expedition slowly struggled up the steep rock path leading to the top of Paltz Point (later renamed Sky Top). Once

Founders Albert and Eliza Smiley returning from a walk with guests, c. 1890. Nature walks and hiking have always been a favorite activity of guests.

*Legend has it that "Mohonk" means "lake in the sky," but scholars versed in the Delaware Indian tongue feel it was likely applied to the white rocks or an area at the base of the mountain.

on top, the beauties of the area spread out before the eager eyes of the beholders.

There, in full view, lay the still waters of Mohonk and in the distance the surrounding forest. To the east lay the Wallkill Valley dotted with the checkerboard patterns of farmland; to the west lay the Rondout Valley and the Catskills; and farther to the south, the rolling hills near West Point with the flatter land ultimately leading to New York City ninety miles away. In the farthest reaches of their gaze stretched the lands of five adjacent states.

At top: Alfred and Rachel Smiley, c. 1900. *Above:* Albert Smiley and sister-in-law Effie Smiley, 1904.

Alfred at once recognized the numerous possibilities the lake afforded and believed it was the ideal spot for the summer home that had been part of Albert's plan for his later years. He and his companions decided to spend the evening at a tavern located on the northwest shore of the lake. Smiley engaged Mohonk's owner, John F. Stokes, in conversation concerning possible sale of the lake. Stokes explained to Smiley that he had purchased the lake in 1858. After much expense and time he had opened up a tavern on July 4, 1859, with a grand opening celebration. The grand opening was a success, complete with fistfights and "whiskey in plenty." At present, Stokes found himself in financial straits, and the visit by Alfred Smiley could not have come at a better time.

Alfred Smiley sensed that the splendor of the Shawangunks lay in their individuality, an isolated range that rose out of cultivated valleys, unlike many eastern mountains with gradual

Stokes Tavern—Currier and Ives, c. 1865. Currier and Ives described itself as "publishers of cheap and popular prints" and left a legacy of more than a million lithograph prints popular in America.

slopes, rounded outlines, and broad plateau-like summits. Striking features included precipitous crags, and abrupt, perpendicular, and overhanging quartz rock formations. Much of this "Shongum grit," Alfred observed, was covered with lichens. It was indeed a magnificent area of folded ridges with escarpments and crevices. The 2,000-foot-high Shawangunk ridge thrust upward from the Wallkill Valley, revealing magnificent vistas.

All around the lake Alfred could see beauty and the potential for enhancement. Here, gleaming quartz crystals shone and olive-colored lichen clusters cast dark patterns; there, the glossy green hues of the laurel contrasted with the white stone; all about were hills covered with pine, hemlock, and chestnut. Though a devastating forest fire in 1864 left scars on trees

Mohonk House 1870. A view alongside of the tavern looking toward Sky Top. W. T. Weaver painted this watercolor in 1908, copying an 1870 photograph.

around Mohonk Lake, Alfred was able to look beyond the unkempt conditions and envision the many possibilities for beautification and ornamentation. The tavern, by comparison one of the finest in the New Paltz area, needed improvements.

"The owner was John F. Stokes, an old man of high personal character but without education," recalled Albert Smiley in his 1904 Parlor talk:

> He was simple in his habits, and he had had the good sense to buy a number of tracts of land here at a very low price. He had a little tavern where he entertained day parties and had a hall where parties from the valleys could come up and dance. One large room was used for this purpose. Overhead were ten bedrooms, seven by five feet. He also sold liquor. Whenever anyone wanted dinner, he and an Irish lad caught a chicken and killed it right in front of the house and an old woman did the cooking. The beds were like the bunks in a steamer, and each bedroom had one chair. The neighbors came up here and had a jolly good time doing about as they wanted to. … When anyone got drunk or hard to manage, Stokes used to chain them to trees, so that he did maintain order in a way.

A description of Mohonk by Smiley family friend and attorney Alonzo T. Clearwater bolsters Smiley's impression with this lively account:

> My first visit to Mohonk was in 1867. At that time, Stokes had a small summer house, a portion of which projected over the lake. In the floor was a trap door with two ring bolts. One on the upper surface was used to raise the door. To the ring on the under surface was attached a piece of bedcord. To it in turn was attached a two-gallon jug of Jerry Green's four year old apple whiskey. This jug and its contents furnished the bar of Stokes Tavern, the principle condiment of which to the casual visitor was huckleberry pie. On the occasion of my first visit as a member of a party of ten or twelve, we carried our own luncheon, largely consisting of chicken sandwiches and cake. Stokes contributed huckleberry pie and milk. He had a supply of nutmegs. He opened his bar and suggested milkpunch. The offer was gladly accepted, but the price was somewhat exorbitant.

John Stokes
on Lake Shore
Road, 1870.

That night over dinner, Stokes told Alfred that he had planned to sell the lake and surrounding land to his creditors. Having six children to raise, Alfred was in no financial position to purchase the property from Stokes, but he persuaded the debt-ridden owner to wait
until a telegram could be sent to his brother in Providence. "Await a letter and come on
immediately," wired the anxious Alfred. Albert, in the midst of a busy time of planning at
Friends School for two hundred pupils and eighteen teachers, sent word that he could not
make it. Alfred sent another plea and Albert made plans to journey immediately to Paltz
Point. Alfred entered into more discussion with Stokes.

Upon his arrival at Mohonk, Albert Smiley quickly "fell in love with the scenery and felt sure of its development." Mohonk's environs offered the elixir he sought. Ever since his wife Eliza's breakdown in health following their daughter Nettie's death in March 1863, Albert had been on the lookout for such a location. About the time of Alfred's fateful excursion, Albert noted, "I, too, suffered as severe a case of nervous prostration as I have ever known," brought about by overwork at school.

Stokes asked $40,000 for the 300 acres of land and the lake. Albert left instructions with his brother, before heading back to Providence, urging him to bargain with Stokes. Alfred

Original tavern with paddle wheeler moored on the shore, 1870.

Paddle wheeler anchored out of sight of the Mountain House. This image was published on souvenir stereopticon cards by proprietor Smiley shortly after purchasing Mohonk. These cards with various scenes throughout America became home parlor entertainment.

succeeded in persuading Stokes to lower the price, and the two men agreed upon the sum of $28,000. Albert had $14,000 in savings, the result of twenty years' frugality. Included in the $14,000 was $300 that Eliza Smiley had saved while teaching at Friends School. Albert borrowed the remaining $14,000 and as a result stayed on at Providence to pay his debt. "My sole purpose," stated Smiley, "was to provide a home, and in order to pay for it I started in a business for which, above all things in the world, I had a distaste, and no experience."

At forty-one years of age, Alfred and Albert engaged upon an enterprise in resort ownership that was totally foreign to their upbringing and inclination. "I had no more thought of it than going to the moon," observed Albert. Fortunately, Alfred Smiley was nearby in Poughkeepsie on the farm. The proximity of the farm to Mohonk enabled Albert to stay at Friends School and draw a salary in order to meet the expense of fashioning the future Mohonk Mountain House and grounds.

Fate or destiny often works in wondrous ways, but potential is sensed and grasped only by those prescient and brave enough to dare. And so, Albert Smiley, school administrator, purchased a lake, a tavern, and some rugged terrain. Mohonk afforded the possibility of a summer retreat and a business. Plans for a projected hotel must be laid; the land must be scrutinized, and roads and paths on the property built to permit access to its beauty.

Albert Smiley inherited the paddle wheeler from Stokes when he purchased the lake. He said: "Stokes had two little boats and a larger boat with a wheel on it. Often visitors were ferried across from the other side in this boat. We kept it around for some time and then scuttled it and sank it in the lake." In a later talk, Albert described this old boat with a wheel on it. "By turning the crank they used to propel it and this was the way they had of ferrying people across from the other side of the lake."

Throughout the nineteenth century until the 1880s, with the introduction of swimwear on a large scale to accommodate changing societal attitudes about nudity, men and boys customarily swam naked. Former archivist Joan LaChance wrote that the paddle wheeler "brought men to the swimming area cove—the exact same spot where the swimming area is today—but you couldn't walk to it then, and it was not visible from the tavern."

Frederick Partington in *The Story of Mohonk** captured Alfred's emotions:

To the man who had just climbed the mountain and stood enraptured on the other side of the lake, it was a prospect for which he could imagine no bounds. He saw in that quick sweep of his eye the whole future of the place unfolding and forming. He could scarcely believe that business sagacity had thus far missed a chance like this. He was standing less than a hundred miles from the metropolis of the country; he was surrounded by romantic natural features absolutely unknown to the great outside world—and so unique in character that they could be brought into no comparison with any other known region of the eastern states. ∾

Frederick Partington wrote The Story of Mohonk *in 1911. An educator and good family friend of the Smileys, Partington had planned to rewrite his story, but died in 1924 before he could do so. Subsequent editions retained the original Partington text with updated additions by later Smileys.*

2

Creating the Mountain House

"He and I always thought alike. ... We had many of our interests in common."

Albert K. Smiley, speaking of his brother Alfred

The wisest decision Albert made was to induce his twin brother to oversee the operation at Mohonk and manage it until a permanent move could be made from Providence. Alfred Smiley lived in Poughkeepsie, less than twenty miles from Mohonk. He possessed sound business sense and complemented his brother well. During the winter and spring of 1870, the tavern was remodeled to accommodate forty guests. Verandas were added, roads and paths were surveyed and cut in the forest; the Mohonk Mountain House was ready for occupancy on June 1st.

William Burgess, hired by Alfred to be the first manager of the Mohonk Mountain House, proved inapt for the job. Lamenting this fact, Alfred observed that Burgess "knew very little about running a hotel and in those days a hotel man was hardly considered respectable." Respectable or not, Alfred became resigned to personnel eccentricities and saw to the steady improvement of the guest facilities. Albert meanwhile determined that Alfred should manage the next year, thus beginning an association and family involvement that was to grow in future years.

One of the most demanding projects for 1870 was the improvement of the road along the shore of the lake. Tree stumps had been used as a water fill for the roadbed, but after many decades holes developed as the stumps rotted. Although improvements were slow for Albert's ambitious plans, the creation of the Mohonk resort, and especially the "Mohonk spirit," left a formation not unlike the durable Shawangunks themselves. Plans, ideas, concepts—molded, tried, and remolded—eventually fused and like stone conglomerate were ready to withstand the vicissitudes of the world, determined to persevere.

The first forty guests at the Mountain House were nearly all personal friends from Philadelphia and New York. Thus the simple quarters were soon filled with paying guests, even though most were at the same time personal friends. Albert loved to have his friends around him, and they delighted in the opportunity of spending a summer in such a beautiful place with congenial company.

One of the good fortunes was the arrival at Mohonk of Schuyler Colfax, Vice President of the United States. Colfax, an affable and likeable man, was as yet untouched by his role in the Credit Mobilier scandal. From the first Mohonk information circular, April 14, 1870, is this account: "Vice President Colfax, who visited the place last summer with a party of friends, spoke of it enthusiastically as reminding him of the wonderful rock and valley views of the Yosemite Valley, in California, and in a letter addressed to the proprietor, dated Washington, March 27, 1870, says: 'I was delighted with my visit to Paltz Point [Sky Top], with Mr. Cornell, and regarded the scenery there as most beautiful and picturesque—far more beautiful, indeed, than I had anticipated.'" This was among the first of many such testimonials, which would attract a well-to-do, educated clientele.

The Smileys decided to run their hotel operation along strictly Quaker lines. The liquor question was an easily determined policy at Mohonk. As Quakers, Alfred and Albert were temperance advocates, and so temperance ruled at Mohonk. Stokes urged the brothers to reconsider their decision and suggested that they put in a bar and race track. Stokes was certain that the Smileys' venture would lose money and end in defeat without liquor. Despite Stokes's doubt and air of local skepticism, the Smileys not only banned alcohol but card playing and dancing as well. Those activities were replaced by a voluntary ten-minute prayer service after breakfast each morning, daily nature walks, lectures, evening concerts, golf (later), bowling, boating, horseback riding, fishing, a church service on Sunday (nondenominational) and an evening hymn-sing, and an emphasis on conversation with others and direct contact with nature.

From the outset the Smileys believed that people should come to the mountains for a respite from the rigors and routine of city life. Why, they asked, engage people in the same activities common in the city? While none of the Mohonk guests was compelled to attend the morning worship service, many did take part.

Albert, holding a Smiley family prayer book, leading daily prayers in the Old Parlor, c. 1890.

Right: Guests driving a carriage past the garden, c. 1900.

Below: A Mohonk driver brings his four-horse tally-ho down Whitney Road after an excursion in 1936.

Opposite page: This hand-tinted photograph shows horseback riders enjoying the scenic Rondout Valley, 1932.

Photo: Daniel Smiley, Jr.

In the early years of Mohonk's development, the Smileys' concern for people's relationship with one another and to nature became firmly established. Conversation, quiet, and concerts helped to promote friendships, while nature walks, hikes, and drives encouraged visitors to understand nature more fully. Horses provided a means by which guests could appreciate the splendid surroundings whether by small carriage, four-horse tally-ho, or horseback. In this way they fashioned a resort where the guest could feel free from his cares and become invigorated by the bracing air, vivid scenery, and contact with some of the finest minds in America.

For Alfred Smiley the managing of Mohonk proved to be a full-time task. For the first two years he continued to plant his crops on the farm in Poughkeepsie, and during the summer he traveled there once a week. Alfred's sons, Edward, Fred, and George, and a hired hand did most of the farm labor. Finally, Alfred was forced to cease farming in 1872 in order to devote

his complete attention to the rapidly expanding business at Mohonk. During the winter of 1872, when Mohonk was closed and when much of the repair work and road construction was taking place, Alfred hired a steward, Colonel James Smith (a brother of William and Andrew Smith of Smith Brothers' cough drop fame) to help in the operations.

Alfred proved to be an excellent manager. While the twin brothers got on well together, Alfred at times became vexed by Albert's lack of business sense. "With all the conclusions to which thee seems to have come I do not at all agree," Alfred admonished Albert in a November 1872 letter. "Whether thee wants to enlarge the number of boarders or not it seems to me imperatively needed many better rooms." Urging that Albert realize that profits are large during the season but "the expenses last all the year round," he reminded Albert of the necessity to improve the rooms. Some guests preferred certain rooms, while a Mrs. Jones accepted Number 29 under protest. Moreover, Alfred noted that an enlargement to the house must be undertaken at once. The final thrust of Alfred's arguments underscored the problem: "Next season thee will have all the expenses of a first class house & has had no hesitation about adding expensive kitchen & water closet arrangements & yet does hesitate at the only point where an increased revenue may be expected. These matters seem very clear to me and I wonder thee doesn't see them too."

During the decade of the 1870s, building and grounds improvement was a priority, with Alfred Smiley favoring the former and Albert pushing for the latter. The house was enlarged in 1871 to accommodate more guests. A telegraph office for the convenience of guests, and especially for the reservations office, was installed in 1873. Increased patronage led to construction of the Dining Room Building in 1874.

House Construction

In addition to the Dining Room Building, a stone bathroom building and an expansive wooden building called the Long Building were constructed in 1874. This more than doubled the guest occupancy potential and provided for large public spaces. The Long Building also had a viewing platform along the rooftop. In the following year the Garden Wing was added, at the edge of the present putting green. The laundry and icehouse were enlarged, and the lake for the first time stocked with fish—2,000 smallmouth bass.

1890s Employees

In the 1870s, when Mohonk was a new venture, owner Albert Smiley instructed his brother Alfred to see about recruiting kitchen, dining room, and laundry help from among the staff at nearby Vassar College. Because Mohonk opened for the summer months when the college was not in session, this was an advantageous arrangement. The Smileys also recruited from local populations for these positions, notably from the hamlet of Kyserike.

The executive division of the business was comprised of the front office staff and the head managers. Archival documents refer to employees—many ladies and one gentleman—carrying out administrative duties in the front office. These included front desk assistance, recording of arrivals, addressing and sending annual brochures and calendars and answering letters from potential guests, bookings and refusals, keeping card records and files, stenography, conference arrangements, conference reports, and bookkeeping.

At top: Kitchen crew, 1893. *Above:* Front office staff, 1890s.

In 1876 the bowling saloon with four alleys was constructed and used for that recreation through the 1950s. It is Mohonk's oldest outbuilding still standing. When it became the Council House in 1960, it served a variety of groups for meetings, activities, and religious services. In more recent decades it has served diverse purposes including as a ski shop, craft house, and center for kids' club activities.

Closing out the 1870s decade of bustling construction, in 1879 the Rock Building was added on to the existing Mountain House building sections—notably perched atop the cliff face known as Pine Bluff. Significant blasting was done to level the site for construction. It remains as the oldest existing section of the Mountain House and adjoins the newest building section—the Spa Wing.

Long Building, pictured on a stereoptic card, c. 1875.

Photo: J. Loeffler

Rock Building, on far left in 1881 photo, constructed in 1879 and named for the rock cliff on which it was built.

Road Construction

Roads, because of their function and their scenic possibilities, fascinated the Smiley twins.
A curve here, a vista there, a sloping descent into a wooded arbor—it did not matter that
the straight line is the shortest distance between two points. Fortunately for Mohonk, this
unusual blend of aesthetic temperament and skillful use of surveying instruments created a
wonderland of carriage roads and paths and trails for walking. In subsequent decades jog-
ging, cross-country skiing, and mountain biking also used the carriage roads.

Right: Road construction, 1900. The steep terrain necessitated using hand tools to further break apart the large chunks of conglomerate rock blasted from the cliff walls.

Below: Garden Road construction, 1924. Dynamite and steam-powered drills were used to break apart the dense rock terrain.

Photo: Albert K. Smiley, II

Photo: Albert K. Smiley, II

Laurel Ledge
Road. Vertical
cliff faces were
particularly
challenging to
cut into.

During the first fifty years of proprietorship, the Smileys developed an impressive network of carriage roads winding through the thousands of acres of scenic ridge top and forest lands that surround the Mountain House. These carriage roads were built with labor-intensive methods, using picks, shovels, wheelbarrows, crowbars, sledgehammers, stone boats, horses, a hand-cranked derrick, and a portable steam engine. Two of the earliest roads constructed were Eagle Cliff Road and Woodland Drive, completed in 1872. They remain highly popular hiking routes for guests today. The Mohonk carriage road network eventually totaled 110 miles. ❧

Garden Road construction, 1924. Workers were hired from the nearby Wallkill and Rondout Valleys.

Photo: Albert K. Smiley, II

3

By Word of Mouth and in Print: Nineteenth-Century Advertising

*"I want you to pack your trunk and paintbox and come right off
to Poughkeepsie to go with me and enjoy a few weeks sketching
at Lake Mohunk* [sic], *as picturesque a place as I ever saw."*

Henry van Ingen

As the amenities of the Mountain House and the striking natural features became more accessible, the reputation of Mohonk was spread by enthusiastic guests. The Smiley brothers did not believe in formal advertising, preferring to have a more direct relationship with their guests. For many years word-of-mouth advertising was relied upon. The Lake Mohonk Mountain House brochure stood as a rare exception, employing printed advertisement. Published yearly, these brochures described the facilities, listed the prices, and contained selected comments by former guests or newspaper reporters. Advertising may not have been used officially by the Smileys, yet Alfred's son Edward recalls that Albert Leroy stayed in the fall and early winter of 1873 and worked outside, and in January he went to New York and handed out small one-page circulars by ringing doorbells from Canal Street to Central Park.

The 1874 brochure contained brief statements describing the Smiley attitude toward advertising: "From the first opening of the house four years ago, the plan has been steadily continued to employ no correspondents, and never, directly or indirectly, to solicit any newspaper notices whatever." Among the favorable comments were those from a number of prominent people. Arnold Guyot, the first Professor of Geography and Geology at Princeton University, visited Mohonk several times before 1887. Guyot's well-known statement appeared in the 1884 Mohonk publication: "Few spots on our continent unite so much beauty of scenery, both grand and lovely, within so small a compass, to be enjoyed with so much ease." Dr. Howard Crosby, Chancellor of the University of New York, added, "You have done a good service in calling public attention to a spot so romantic, so varied in its scenery, so health-invigorating, and withal so accessible; and you have added to the good service by making one's stay at Mohonk so comfortable, I may even say so luxurious."

Such panegyric might appear gratuitous, yet it was genuinely felt and honestly expressed by thousands of satisfied guests as Mohonk continued. By appealing to a specific class of people who shared similar ideals with Mohonk's owners, the Mohonk Mountain House became independent of the rapid changes or fads that frequently swept through society. With such a

An artist at work, with Albert Smiley observing both the view and the image on the canvas, c. 1890.

background of self-imposed privacy, the Smileys maintained a paying business and relied on the constant patronage of upper-class families, mostly from the East Coast area. The result was a remarkable blend of forces, social and environmental, that caused Mohonk to gain in reputation as a resort of charm and culture.

In the early nineteenth century, years before the Smileys purchased Stokes's Tavern, residents from the hamlets at the foot of the mountain explored Mohonk Lake and cliffs via rough roads and narrow paths. Visiting artists were attracted by Mohonk's dramatic scenery, including notable Hudson River School artists Thomas Cole, William Hart, Thomas Worthington Whittredge, Sanford Robinson Gifford, and others. Once the Smileys opened for business at Mohonk, they were quick to foster connections with artists who had created impressive oil paintings of their new property. These paintings became an ideal means to further Mohonk's reputation and attract new guests.

Alfred recognized that advertising and the hotel identity were indivisible partners. In the first year of operation, he approached notable guests (including Vice President of the United States Schuyler Colfax), knowing that these testimonials would provide effective advertising. One of the first artists Alfred approached was Henry van Ingen, asking him to create a letter that could be quoted in a circular distributed to potential guests.

The letter from van Ingen not only praised Mohonk's setting, but revealed the artist's eye for subjects:

I want you to pack your trunk and paintbox and come right off to Poughkeepsie to go with me and enjoy a few weeks sketching at Lake Mohunk [*sic*], as picturesque a place as I ever saw. Its wildness reminds me most of the scenery we used to admire in Norway, and as for its being healthy, a condition you are so particular about, you will get plenty of fresh air here, the hotel being situated near the top of the mountain and on the bank of the lake.

... after ascending for about two miles, one begins to catch glimpses of this most romantic of lakes. It is surrounded by bold rocks, which for the greater part rise perpendicular from the surface of the water to a height of from twenty to one hundred feet, all covered with dark brown lichen. You can reach the top of the mountain, about 300 feet above the lake, by following a footpath, founded on one side by these

Henry van Ingen's painting *Lake Mohonk,* c. 1865, was created before Albert Smiley purchased the property in 1869. Van Ingen was the founding professor of Vassar College's art department.

dark rocks, rising in isolated masses of stupendous size and assuming all the varied forms of ruined towers of gigantic structure, the chasms separating them appearing of awful depth, while their bases are shrouded in the shades of the forest.

Just now the laurel is in blossom and grows in the richest luxuriance here, often taking root in the narrowest cliffs and crevices of the rocks, showing to greater advantage against their dark color. Come soon and I will be greatly surprised if you don't stay some weeks, fill your portfolio with valuable sketches and leave with mind and body improved by the splendid scenery and invigorating air of this mountain retreat.

One of the most quoted guest testimonials was from Daniel Huntington, a prominent artist long associated with Mohonk.

It is believed that Huntington was the first artist to portray Mohonk Lake and its environs. In his speech given at the Parlor dedication in 1899, he describes his first visit of 1837, when the path up the mountain was nearly impassable with brush and fallen trees:

It was a dark day and the lake looked like a deep dark lake, and we were almost terrified by the grandness of the scenery. Mr. Ver Bract had a flute which he used as a cane, and as we stood there he played up on that flute, and the last notes came back with such sweetness that it thrilled me, and I said to Mr. Ver Bract, the time will come when this place will be a great resort for people of culture, and a large hotel will be built here. I will say, I made a sketch, there was little time to stay as it was getting dark. I will not forget walking through those woods, they were almost primeval forests. We found on the lake a small raft of logs, and there was no house within

Lake Mohonk by Daniel Huntington. The painting was likely a gift from the artist to Mohonk.

two miles, I think. I got on the little boat and tried to paddle about, but it soon went under the water and I came ashore, as I wanted to have an opportunity to paint the picture, and the next winter I painted a general view of the place from recollection, there was not time to make much of a sketch, and it was accepted by the Academy of Design* and was sold there for a sum which was quite a little fortune to me at that time, sixty dollars.

There has been a historical reference to Huntington "up in his studio in this Rock-building ... at work this morning at his easel—holding a steady brush at the age of eighty-three!" It has been noted that after his visits he would ask the head clerk to ship painted canvasses to his New York City home. He would leave his easels, blank canvasses, and supplies at Mohonk to be stored over the winter.

Although he was a confirmed proponent of the family outing, Alfred Smiley, as Mohonk's manager, had little spare time for such pleasures. In the summer of 1876, however, he arranged to take his family and the Albert Smileys on a picnic to Peterskill Falls, a few miles southwest of Mohonk. The driver of their carriage pointed to the top of a mountain towering above the Peterskill and told them of a lake on top. The lake was called Coxing Pond (originally spelled Coxen); the driver offered to show the group the path leading to the top. Alfred, his sons, and Albert readily accepted the driver's offer, and the party followed him up a rocky, narrow pathway. Upon reaching the top of the mountain, Alfred and his sons and Albert beheld a magnificent setting. There lay a lake, somewhat larger than Mohonk, with sparkling water the color of lapis lazuli. The rock cliffs surrounding the lake were striking and sheer, intermittently covered with thick foliage. In order to obtain a better perspective, Alfred climbed a tree to see what the outlook presented. The view was similar to that to be seen from Mohonk, and Sky Top could be seen seven miles to the north.

Alfred immediately inquired as to the owner of Coxing Pond and found that it belonged to George Davis, who lived not far away in the Trapps hamlet. After traveling the two miles from Coxing Pond to the Trapps, Alfred stopped on his way home to see Davis and planned

*Daniel Huntington was president of the National Academy of Design from 1862 to 1870, and again from 1877 to 1890. He was also vice president of the Metropolitan Museum of Art.

4

Another Brother and a Change for Mohonk

"He is twenty-seven years my junior and always seems to me more like a son than a brother."

Albert K. Smiley, speaking of his half-brother Daniel

Two events occurred in 1879 that permanently influenced the future of Mohonk: the decision of Albert to offer his younger brother a position in the business, thus selecting a successor; and Albert's appointment by President Rutherford B. Hayes as a member of the United States Board of Indian Commissioners.

Daniel Smiley was born in the family home in Vassalboro, Maine, on November 29, 1855. His father Daniel had married Dorcas Hanson after his first wife's death. A half-brother to Alfred and Albert, Daniel was twenty-seven years younger. His early life in Maine bore similarity to that spent by his older brothers. Daniel also did his schoolwork while clearing stones from his father's fields, and that afforded him ample time to master his lessons. "The stones seemed to grow faster than the potatoes which I planted," Daniel later declared. After attending the Oak Grove Seminary across the way from the Smiley farm, he entered Haverford College. Following graduation in 1878, Daniel went to Philadelphia where he served as an instructor of Latin and Greek. He also served as assistant principal at the William Penn Charter School. When Albert first suggested a move to Mohonk, Daniel was completing work on a Greek grammar.

It was no easy decision for Daniel to leave his position as a teacher and embark upon a new and unfamiliar life as manager of a resort hotel. After much discussion with his brother, he accepted the invitation to move to Mohonk in June of 1881 when he was twenty-five years of age. Albert and Eliza, without children of their own, came to look upon him as their son. They were pleased that the younger brother and his family reciprocated their affection and shared their goals. Early in his stay at Mohonk, Daniel demonstrated that his talents were ideally suited to his new environment and that he would provide the business acumen missing since Alfred's departure. He became a willing and able partner in the continuing development of Mohonk.

"He is scholarly and honest and I could trust him," remarked Albert when discussing Daniel's talents. "I had him spend the summer before he was married with me," he recalled, "and I used to take a walk with him … ." The walks turned out to be more than pleasant interludes. Albert was testing Daniel to see whether his younger brother had the taste to lay out a road or spot a scenic view. "'What a pretty place,' he would say," observed Albert, "and I saw he had good judgment of what was good in nature and art." Before he induced Daniel to come to Mohonk, Albert sought the consent of his brother's future wife. "And she has gone in the bargain,"

Daniel Smiley, c. 1880.

noted Albert. Daniel's wife Effie became Albert's private secretary and Mohonk's hostess. "When I get in my dotage," concluded Albert in assessing Daniel's role, "he will take my place, and he is taking it rapidly." That remark made by Albert Smiley in 1899 came seven years after he had already given Daniel full charge of Mohonk's operations.

Daniel's wife, Effie Newell of China, Maine, was an Oak Grove Seminary schoolmate of Daniel's and lent much graciousness to the Mohonk tradition. She provided encouragement and advice to her husband and her brother-in-law.

Once settled at the Mohonk Mountain House in 1881, Daniel arranged to teach at the local academy in New Paltz during the winter. The New Paltz atmosphere exuded its seventeenth-century Dutch and French heritage, and the Dutch language was still being taught when Daniel arrived there. "I am happy and glad to have this opportunity to say before you all," Daniel declared in his response at the 1899 dedication of the parlor, "what I do not know that I have ever said to my brother, that I am exceedingly glad for the pleasant experiences and the many, many happy days that I have had here with him." He also noted that he was grateful for Albert's urging him to come to Mohonk. "I think perhaps I can do some good instructing others," said Daniel; "perhaps there is a chance here to satisfy myself in as great an extent as in the professional life." Like Albert, Daniel remained interested and involved in educational work for the rest of his life. His service to a number of college boards of trustees on the East Coast and in the West indicated an intense dedication to his former profession.

Smiley family members Mary Cornell (Eliza's sister), Effie, Eliza, Bert (Daniel and Effie's oldest son), Albert, and Daniel, c. 1885.

As the manager of Mohonk, Daniel Smiley evidenced shrewd business sense. Recognizing the importance of his staff, Daniel followed Albert's philosophy of nurturing promising employees. As Albert had proudly remarked in his 1899 Parlor dedication speech:

We take bell boys and advance them, and they are soon regular clerks. Our head cook was night watchman and he is going down to Lakewood for the winter. Our head waiter was trained in here, and we train all our men from the ranks. The

Porters, pictured here in 1897, facilitated transportation of guests and baggage—often transporting numerous large steamer trunks, since many guests stayed for extended periods.

steward is one of Moloy's boys, grown up here, and in winter manages a large hotel in Florida, and some of our clerks and other employees are going down with him. Our head farmer has been here twenty years, a very good man, and we always hold on to a good man when we can, and the man who has charge of our mechanical works, was brought up as a bell boy, he trained himself by studying, and we recognize men by their merit. And we have no men from New York City with their prejudices. Our people work for us and we try to treat them well, and they do good service for us.

Daniel also pioneered the idea among his employees and his family that, since the hotel was away from the city, "we must not get 'stuck' in any emergency ... we have learned to depend on ourselves. ..." Daniel was responsible for making the Mohonk estate self-sufficient in everything from power and heat to soap and food. When electricity was first introduced at Mohonk, electric lights were installed in the Mountain House using generating equipment housed in a nearby building. When Mohonk completed its powerhouse in 1901, an electrical generating system was installed, providing Mohonk's direct current electrical power through 1964.

With the ability to envision and create like Albert, Daniel also served as a steadying force to his brother's prodigious undertakings. One of his finest qualities was his sense of purpose, his careful stewardship over the land and human relations of Mohonk. He could admire his brother's visions and grand goals and at the same time give careful scrutiny to the necessary details and financial backing for such projects. He was a rare example of the practical and the ideal

Bellmen had many responsibilities, including all deliveries to guest rooms such as baggage, firewood, ice water, and food service.

in harmonious blend. His devotion to the works and ideals of his brother Albert and to the standards set by Alfred was nurtured often at personal loss of time and money. Daniel was the preserver who made it possible for the Smiley philanthropies of ensuing years to exist and for the Mohonk spirit to continue. Daniel's daughter, Ruth, recalled that her "Uncle Albert always wanted things done right now and could not understand why the plants could not grow faster. My father would remind him that all things were accomplished in good time." ∽

Powerhouse steam engines, providing direct current electric power, early 1900s.

5

The Conferences

"It would be most deplorable if this house should ever acquire the mercenary spirit and make the accumulation of money without higher ulterior aims the goal of its ambition."

Albert K. Smiley,
dedication of the Testimonial Gateway, October 14, 1908

Albert Smiley, a member of the Religious Society of Friends (Quakers), was steeped in a tradition of concern for social problems and their solution. American Quakers were active in the movement for the abolition of slavery. The Underground Railroad was established with Quaker help. After the Civil War, Quakers were instrumental in efforts to aid freedmen. From the earliest colonial days they had boldly defended Native American Indians' right to a full life. With such a spirit of social activism it is little wonder that Friend Albert Smiley would find it necessary to do his part in seeking an end to previous hostile federal policy toward Indians and replacing it with a more enlightened one of peace and ultimate citizenship for Native Americans.

In the winter of 1879, Albert attended the annual meeting of the Board of Indian Commissioners in Washington, D.C. "Charges of corruption were made at that meeting against certain officers of the Indian Bureau by one of the members of the board," he recalled, "and a committee of the board was appointed to investigate them, of which I was made chairman." Careful investigation by him netted evidence against the three men, and Secretary of the Interior Carl Schurz dismissed them from the Indian service. Schurz then called upon the board to investigate the whole Bureau of Indian Affairs. Smiley was again made chairman of the investigating committee. He later recalled that he "inspected the whole Indian Bureau, and particularly its methods of doing business. ... This is how I came at once to be deeply interested in Indian work."

One aspect of Indian affairs that disturbed Smiley was the lack of coordination in planning among people who sought to solve the "Indian question," as it was then known. The many organizations, public and private, had little or no communication with each other. It had been the practice of the Board of Indian Commissioners to invite the secretaries of all the religious denominations having charge of Indian work to Washington, D.C., once each year. For one day in joint session, reports of fieldwork and Indian affairs were discussed. "One short day seemed to me," noted Smiley, "totally insufficient time to thoroughly complete the discussion, and I tried in vain to have the meeting prolonged."

During an inspection tour of the Santee Sioux Agency in Dakota Territory, Smiley found himself frustrated over the difficult conditions for thorough discussions. He announced to a group of colleagues, "We will finish this discussion at Mohonk Lake, next fall." "I invited them all," he later noted, "to meet at Mohonk the ensuing autumn, and promised to have a large gathering to discuss the whole Indian question."

Lake Mohonk Conferences of Friends of the Indian: Discussing Native American Matters

"The service of the Lake Mohonk Conferences to the cause of Indian advancement can hardly be overemphasized." Loring Benson Priest, 1942

In 1883 invitations to the first annual Lake Mohonk Conference of Friends of the Indian were sent to fifty people, including the Board of Indian Commissioners. The conference met in October as guests of Albert Smiley and his wife. Smiley suggested that the Board of Indian Commissioners could meet officially at the same time. That was a shrewd maneuver because it allowed the Mohonk Conference reports to be printed in the board's subsequent annual reports.

It also made sure that all the commissioners mingled with the nation's leading figures in Indian affairs amidst the congenial and beautiful surroundings of Mohonk. Albert considered it a matter of primary urgency "that those representing the Indian cause should arrive at clear and definite conclusions regarding the object to be attained, that the conference should be plainly set before the public in printed form, and as widely circulated as possible."

The conference chairmen were selected by Albert and possessed views generally in line with the host's goals. Yet Albert did not dictate to the conference. By selecting a presiding officer who possessed tact and diplomacy and who could cut off desultory discussion, Smiley silently guided the conference participants in seeking tangible goals rather than spleen-venting accusations. As the yearly meetings continued at Mohonk, concepts were formulated and disseminated, and the conferences exerted increasingly wide influence. From 1883 to 1916, they played a significant role in the formation of United States Indian policies. Wrote author and Indian affairs scholar Loring Benson Priest, "Out of their sessions came programs which subsequently inspired much criticism, but which then represented the majority thinking of friends of the Indian. The policies they recommended were those which guided administration of Indian affairs during the next quarter century."

The high-minded sentiments and spirited discussions that characterized the conferences were followed by a chance for delegates to relax and mull over the proceedings. The conferences opened their sessions at 10 AM, adjourned for lunch at noon, and resumed at 8 PM after dinner. The early morning was left open for free time and wandering about the estate. The afternoons were often taken up with a longer carriage ride or trip to nearby Minnewaska. So enjoyable was the 1884 journey to Minnewaska that the evening session was late in starting because the delegates did not return from their pleasant trip until after dark. Such a schedule permitted debate without fatigue and loss of temper arising from overly long sessions.

The Mohonk Indian conferences brought together prominent white men and women from all aspects of concern for Indian affairs. Smiley invited secretaries of all the religious societies, the Senate and House Committees on Indian Affairs, army officers having dealings with Indians, members of the Bureau of Indian Affairs, heads of Indian schools, members of the Indian Rights Association and Women's National Indian Association, leading newspaper editors, and philanthropists. Complex social conditions and the then prevailing sentiment that white people could best create a government policy toward Indians precluded Native American speakers until the 1889 conference. A random sampling of names in attendance at the conferences indicates not only the type of influential delegate but also the fact that many were frequent guests at Mohonk: Generals N.A. Miles, O.O. Howard, Clinton B. Fisk, and John Eaton; publishers Edwin Ginn and Henry O. Houghton; businessmen John Arbuckle,

Attendees of the 1899 Lake Mohonk Conference of Friends of the Indian posed on the Parlor Porch. Effie Smiley is in the white dress, seated in the front row, and Albert Smiley is standing in the back row, third from the right.

John D. Rockefeller, and Darwin R. James; clergymen Lyman Abbott, Theodore L. Cuyler, Bishop H.B. Whipple, and Cardinal James Gibbons; political and government leaders Attorney General Charles J. Bonaparte, Senator Henry L. Dawes, and former President Rutherford B. Hayes; university president Andrew D. White; authors and magazine publishers Samuel June, Isabel Barrows, Edward Everett Hale, and William Hayes Ward; and reformers Samuel C. Armstrong, Alice C. Fletcher, Richard H. Pratt, Amelia S. Quinton, and Herbert Welsh.

After 1889, Indian leaders invited to address the conferences included Dr. Charles Eastman, Dr. Carlos Montezuma, Chester Cornelius, the Revered Sherman Coolidge, and Chapman Scanandoah. They expressed their opinions and mingled with the members. Often Indian pupils from various schools were guests. A few listed on the membership rolls and who spoke include J. DuBray, Hattie Longwolf, Dennison Wheelock, Samuel George, and Francis LaFlesche.

When the chairman rang his "five-minute bell" for the last time at the 1916 Lake Mohonk conference, it marked the end of a thirty-three-year campaign for government reform in Indian affairs. As a personal effort, the conferences reflect through their records and reports the unselfish and dedicated humanitarianism of Albert and Daniel Smiley. As a public event, the conferences represented the coalition of a remarkable and diverse group of influential men and women into a unified whole striving at Mohonk to secure a better life for the Indians. To Smiley and his associates it seemed wrong for the United States to segregate Indians on reservations, to deny them citizenship and, above all, to prevent them from sharing in American culture.

In the first decade of the conferences, spokespeople with strains of ethnocentrism favored Dawes's Severalty Act, allotting reservation land into farms and selling the surplus for a trust fund to advance education and health care for Native Americans. By the second decade, such certitude became hotly debated, and a strong sentiment emerged favoring Indian cultural and religious preservation.

Mohonk's efforts were unflagging. Charitable funds were solicited at the conferences to pay for legal protection for the Mission Indians, the Pueblos, the Pimas, and the Alaskan natives. Some of the Mohonk guests provided scholarships to send young Indians to college. The conferences underwrote the "Mohonk Lodge" at Colony, Oklahoma, and a pottery works at Laguna, New Mexico, that provided direct educational, cultural, and medical benefits for the Indians. By underwriting legal fees, the conferences played a major role in securing reservation land for the Mission Indians of Southern California.

Subsequent events proved the policies advocated at Mohonk to be a mixture of success and fail-ure. As an influential group seeking to arouse public and governmental conscience, the conferences were an unqualified success. But after seeking the formal adoption of many of the changes that it had advocated, Mohonk often found itself unable to see to the practical implementation of its theories in the political world of Washington, D.C.

Hopes for sound health, equality of opportunity, and full civil rights stood little chance of fulfillment in the face of political and private resistance to execution of the laws. The political mischief that afflicted the Indian Bureau—admitted by the commissioners and condemned by the crusaders—served to weaken the thrust of Mohonk's reforms. Moreover, looking back from present perspective, we see that some of the reform solutions that it advocated were impracticable, such as the Dawes Severalty Act; certain liberal or avant-garde positions of 1905 later became outmoded cultural notions.

Nevertheless, the work of the Lake Mohonk conferences leaves a legacy worthy of study. In 1883 the predominant tendency of the nation was to ignore or dispossess the Indians, although there was still to be killing ahead, including the Wounded Knee Massacre in 1890. By 1916 the attitude of the public and the government alike had been dramatically altered. Serious concern for education, health, and preparation for citizenship replaced persecution. Compassion and understanding began to supplant indifference and hostility. While historical treatment of Native Americans remains a blot on America's national reputation, a study of the Mohonk conferences reveals that during the period between 1883 and 1916 Albert and Daniel Smiley did much to change United States policy and bring about improvement in the treatment of Indians.

The name "Mohonk" became known throughout the land. In the 1960s the Smiley family transferred the 22,000 items of Indian conference records to Haverford College, where they are now used by researchers and students of American history.

A 1983 conference marking the centennial of the Lake Mohonk Conferences of Friends of the Indian. It featured leading historians and Native American elders from across the country.

Mohonk Conferences on the Negro Question: Addressing African American Conditions

"At its heart, the Negro Question is white racial preju-dice, and consequently whites, not blacks, were in need of education." Albion W. Tourgée

Once Albert Smiley had established conferences to address Native American policy, he sought to apply the same blueprint to address other issues facing the nation. In 1890 the first Mohonk Conference on the Negro Question was held. Albert Smiley invited more than one hundred prominent religious, educational, political, and philanthropic leaders to Mohonk to discuss, as it was then called, "The Negro Question." During the twenty-five years following the end of the Civil War, African American citizens continued to suffer from lynchings, restricted rights, extreme racial prejudice, and paternalistic attitudes.

Albert Smiley was notably ahead of his time in sponsoring this audacious gathering focusing on an explosive subject. He asked his sister, Sarah Smiley—a fervent activist and human rights advocate—to be one of the featured speakers. In her presentation she recounted her efforts to aid African Americans: "Just at the close of the war I gave about three years of my life to this cause; and I look back upon them as those which educated *me* most, whatever they did for the Negro, they were so rich in experience. I went to relieve human suffering; but I soon found myself drawn into this very line of work that has come before us this morning, and which seems to me the solution of the problem." She

went on to explain the ways in which she offered aid to these people—whom she described as refugees—many of whom were left in extreme poverty.

Despite the Quaker sentiment to aid African Americans in their plight, the overall climate in this country was such that legal separation of the races continued to be the law of the land. This was exem-plified, just a few years later in 1896, by the Supreme Court case *Plessy v. Ferguson*, which upheld the con-stitutionality of racial segregation.

Attending the 1890 Mohonk conference was Albion W. Tourgée (a long-ago carpetbagger and nov-elist), uncompromising critic of white racism, and unswerving supporter of equitable national aid to edu-cation. He stunned his audience by noting that only white people were at the conference and identifying race prejudice as the cause, because many white guests would not appear at a conference attended by Afri-can Americans. Further, he condemned the South's "slave holding mentality," and Northern "do-gooders" for their blindness to injustice in their midst, for their paternalism, and for their assumptions that blacks would be better off for becoming "white at heart." The audience attacked Tourgée vigorously.

But the drama was not over. At the second con-ference, in 1891, A.L. Phillips, Field Secretary for the Colored Evangelization of the Southern Presbyte-rian Church from Tuscaloosa, Alabama, insisted that only Southerners had enlightened and true knowl-edge of race relations, and he reminded "do-gooders" that "unwritten laws" existed in the South forbidding

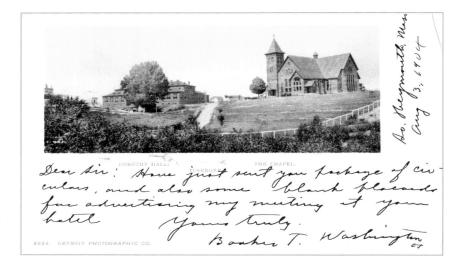

Booker T. Washington writing to Albert K. Smiley, on a Tuskegee Institute picture postcard, in advance of his fundraising visit to Mohonk in 1904.

social mingling of blacks and whites. His plea for formal observance of race separation angered conferees, many of them shouting "never! never!"

The Conferences on the Negro Question could not help but drown in the turbulent political and social times. Jim Crow laws and the Ku Klux Klan were on the rise, and whites were hesitant to broaden African American rights. Their fear of social and political implications thwarted their ability to address issues of prejudice.

Smiley reluctantly pulled the plug. Instead, he turned his own charitable impulses to inviting African American leaders Booker T. Washington and Harry Burleigh to address Mohonk guests and host "pass-the-hat" fundraisers for Tuskegee Institute and other colleges that served African American students.

These long-ago exchanges reflect the contending forces of change. Ethnicity and equal access to the "American dream" remain contentious social issues in the present day, reflecting the conspicuous presence of the past.

Lake Mohonk Conferences on International Arbitration: Seeking a Peaceful World

"A permanent tribunal [for international arbitration of disputes], *I want to urge first, second, last, and always a permanent tribunal. That is the thing … which must be rubbed into the public mind."*
Edward Everett Hale, 1895

Albert Smiley's determination to host yearly conferences on arbitration, despite the wrath and scoffing he might incur from some circles, came from the strongly held conviction that the forces favoring arbitration of disputes among nations should unify their ranks. "It was a happy thought and has yielded rich fruitage," observed Smiley family friend, the Reverend Dr. Theodore L. Cuyler, in assessing the role of the Lake Mohonk Conferences on International Arbitration. As a Quaker, Smiley had long cultivated a desire to seek peace rather than wage war, to arbitrate rather than dictate. He was "impressed in the duty of intelligent and organized propaganda for the attainment of international peace through arbitration." It was in June 1895 that Albert Smiley called the first Mohonk Conference on International Arbitration. The time for such a gathering was in many respects ripe. The United States had been involved in encouraging arbitration of disputes in one form or another since 1871.

As historian Laurence M. Hauptman noted in the Introduction to *Index of the Proceedings of the Lake Mohonk Conferences on International Arbitration 1895–1916* (New York: Clearwater Publishing, 1976):

[the Mohonk Arbitration Conferences] have been credited with having given impetus to the Hague Conference movement; the formation of the big-money peace establishment—the World Peace Foundation and the Carnegie Endowment for International Peace—as well as reconstituting an older one, the New York

Lake Mohonk Conference on International Arbitration, 1902. Albert is seated second from right.

Peace Society; the creation of the American Society of International Law; and the League to Enforce Peace. Historians, contemporary observers and participants have maintained that, besides contributing to the movement for international arbitration, the conferences spawned a furthering of world peace and international understanding, Pan-Americana, Anglo-American amity, and even a version of "Pax Americana." In addition to these interpretations, the conferences served one more fundamental and far-reaching purpose: they were the harbinger and prototype of the modern American foreign policy "think-tank"; the forerunner of such prominent organizations as the Foreign Policy Association and the Council on Foreign Relations. Originating during a decisive period in America's foreign relations, these international forums were the "first publicly organized elite groups in the United States for the regular dissemination of information about broad issues of foreign affairs and the theoretical discussion of foreign policy."

Albert Smiley and dozens of his personally invited guests at the Mohonk conferences believed that the earlier attempts at arbitration were but the groundwork for the successful and permanent implementation of arbitration as a substitute for war. What better country was there to lead in the support of arbitration, the conference delegates asked themselves, than the United States of America?

Lake Mohonk Conference on International Arbitration, 1915.

Lake Mohonk Mountain House

6

"Thistle Pluckers and Rose Planters"

"I have treated this property, the result of seventy-six purchases, as a landscape artist does his canvas, only my canvas covers seven square miles."

Albert K. Smiley, 1907

Albert and Daniel Smiley worked long and hard during the 1880s and 1890s not only to fashion a Mohonk spirit, but also to blend the handiwork of nature with the handiwork of people. Daniel, especially after 1890 when he assumed the management of the Mohonk operation, proved to be a *rara avis* by having the ability of the engineer and the creativity of the artist. As Daniel's grandson, Dan, pointed out, "Mohonk forestry goes back almost to the beginning of scientific forest management in the United States." In the 1900s Albert Smiley would tell his guests that over a thousand cords of wood were cut annually from four square miles of Mohonk forest for the "benefit of the woods." In 1877 Guyot's Hill and Prospect Hill were buckwheat fields. "Most of the trees on those hills were set out by us and are the result of careful forestry," Albert proudly proclaimed.

This emphasis on aesthetics stemmed from the Smileys' concern that visitors to Mohonk be challenged to heighten their perceptions of nature and people's relationship to it. This appreciation for natural beauty channeled much of their effort into the area of "aesthetic forestry." Daniel's grandson Keith wrote, "Through the years, there has ever been the desire to manage our woodlands so as to attain more than one benefit, while making use of the latest forestry techniques."

Albert and Daniel, along with their successors, closely supervised the cutting of views along the more than sixty miles of roads and trails. For example, a vista of the Trapps might be framed by a gnarled tree trunk and colorful foliage. In less accessible wooded areas the

During the 1890s the gardens stretched considerably beyond their current dimensions. A variety of berries, including raspberries, gooseberries, and blackberries, were grown for the enjoyment of guests.

emphasis was placed on a long-range yield of wood for a variety of uses—red oak for furniture (made on the property), plank for road bridges, Christmas trees, wood for fireplaces, poles for the railings, red cedar posts for the Mohonk farm fences, and ash logs to sell for baseball bats.

"I never take a walk or drive over the estate, but I find some ugly tree to be removed, a new path to be built, a group of trees or shrubs to be set out, a vista to be opened, groups of trees to be planted to give seclusion to a too open view, a summerhouse to be built, bright flowers to be set out or dead flowers to be removed," Albert Smiley declared in a statement summarizing the impetus of Mohonk's 7,500-acre landscaping plan.

A 1965 essay by Virginia Smiley in *The Mohonk Bulletin* provides insight into the latest purported phase of aesthetic forestry undertaken by the Smiley family. "At various times during its tenure at Mohonk the Smiley family has been questioned concerning its part in such major projects as the artistic arrangement of the rocks in the Labyrinth across the Lake, and the removal of all the dead laurel blossoms on the property. Our answer is a simple denial of responsibility."

Virginia also wrote: "To an ecologist a dead tree, whether it be standing or lying under a blanket of moss, is just as beautiful as a sprouting seedling or a living tree in full autumn color. Each state of growth and decay is a plan of the tree's destiny, and has a beauty which may only become evident when one is conscious of it as a step in the cycle of life, death, and

rebirth. Is it possible that, through a gain in understanding and appreciation of the natural processes, we searching humans might grow in our relation to the seven ages of man?"

For Albert Smiley the formal flower gardens at Mohonk held a special place in mind and heart. The entire family came to appreciate, and even indulge, his development of gardens. "Thee may charge it to the flower garden" became the byword among the family. Other departments were held closely accountable for expenses, but the Mohonk gardens were and are eval-

Photo: Madeline Smith

From the Victorian era to the present, the whimsical landscape has kindled the imagination and playful spirit of guests.

uated along the lines of pleasure, satisfaction, good health, and beauty—but not in dollars. Daniel's son, Albert, especially favored roses—and lots of them.

As Ruth Smiley wrote in *The Mohonk Garden: A History and Guide,* in 1977:

The Mohonk Gardens reflect primarily the influence of the English style of landscaping during the late nineteenth and early twentieth centuries, and, to a lesser extent, that of the French and Italian styles. Though growing things are never static, the landscape plan still possesses many of the characteristics familiar to that period. An outstanding landscape architect of the late 1800s, Andrew Jackson Downing, lived in nearby Newburgh along the Hudson River. Mr. Downing wrote many books on landscape gardening and was considered one of the leading authorities

The romantic ideal of gardening is captured in this 1916 photograph, emphasizing sweeping vistas to draw the eye gradually from controlled and cultivated flower beds to the rocky, more rugged landscape beyond. Since Mohonk's beginning, arbors and other forms of rustic woodwork have been used to embrace the feeling of being in touch with nature.

Mohonk Lake, N.Y., The Gardens Looking West.

A 1903 postcard of the show garden illustrates the influence of A.J. Downing.

128   The Gardens at Mohonk Lake, N. Y.

This 1930s postcard shows the allure of the gardens with their profusion of vivid blooming flowers.

Taming the Land: Albert Smiley Creates His Garden

The travail and difficulty in planting and caring for the Mohonk gardens, renowned nationwide by aficionados, is best described by Frederick Partington in 1911:

The demolition of the old stables in 1888 marked the real beginning of the extensive gardens. The land thus liberated grew rapidly larger, and, as already mentioned, no one who has not seen the untamable jungle beyond this point could appreciate the combined enthusiasm and energy required to transform all that into the blossoming acres that now stretch almost to the crest of the mountain. What that garden yields in variety and color, what it succeeds in producing against apparently natural obstacles, is a story by itself.

No words can convey any conception of the difficulties that confronted the new owner of Mohonk when he really began to exploit the mountains for roads and flower beds. Gardening, with Mr. Smiley, was dangerously near a passion.

As nature had arranged things at Mohonk there seemed to be only two places for growing flowers—on the quartz rocks and on the branches of trees. A remote third might have been on the lake—a floating garden. There was not a square of a hundred feet where anything but ferns and lichens could hold on—and it had taken some of the lichens a hundred years or more to cover a few

inches. The old guests with records of thirty summers are the only ones who can really appreciate the miracle of the gardens. They can look back to the time when Mr. Smiley used to point with pride to a bed of geraniums on the side of the road close to the water and to a delicate white birch tree that looked like a frail child—not long for this world. He succeeded in stringing those geraniums along the road as it swings over the bridge and to the south, and every bud cost him, probably, five dollars. Anybody caught plucking one would doubtlessly have paid or have been sent away. He classed that sin with drink. Gradually these ganglia of flowers began to grow. Larger beds were made—soil was brought long distances and all around the exterior of the house plants were made to flourish in especially fortified enclosures and in soil that practically had to be renewed to the last particle every year. Finally, when the old stables near the bowling alleys were removed in 1888 the present garden, as already noted, began its remarkable expansion. Beyond the stables lay a wilderness of boulders and cliffs. To civilize this was literally asking Faith to remove mountains. It was done partly, perhaps, to provide space for flowers. It was more likely that the impossible nature of the task acted as a challenge. It is always so with intrepid engineers—pole seekers—besiegers. Getting the land may have been the hardest thing Mr. Smiley ever did—but taming it gave him the greatest delight of his life. He did not rest until he had coaxed into blossom nearly twenty acres of that hopeless slope of the mountain. Most of the earth was brought a mile or more—and the wonder is, still, how it is ever kept in place. To this garden Mr. Smiley has given no end of time and intelligent care, and his reward has been, as he himself says, "a long life and abounding health."

Albert Smiley at the garden entrance arbor, admiring a flower, c. 1910.

of his day. There is no doubt that he had a decided influence on Albert Smiley and his plans for the Mohonk Gardens. The Gardens fit into what Downing described as a "picturesque or romantic style, irregular of form, having variety and boldness of composition, fitting into scenery of wilder picturesque type and abounding in variations of surfaces."

The formal show garden helps to make a gradual and pleasing transition from the Mountain House to the surrounding woodlands. Vine covered arbors and paths invite one beyond the formal show garden areas and lead to a maze, a rose garden, and herb garden, a cutting garden, rock walls, and informal borders, and finally to the naturalistic woodlands.

Landscape gardening of the Victorian era tended toward the naturalistic by encouraging beauty already present. A rocky crag was emphasized by selective pruning; a pool was deepened or ravine cleared to increase its depth, and areas were opened up to invite the long view. An outstanding feature of the Mohonk Gardens is the combination of sweeping lawns and open vistas with stately trees as focal points, surrounded by spectacular rocky cliffs.

Founder Albert Smiley created the overall design, giving shape to an aesthetic tradition for the Mohonk gardens. The gardens continue to reflect his original design, while changing with the tastes of the times and fancies of the head gardeners. ❧

The unique relationship between Mohonk's guests and its owners often occasioned wry comments upon various things. Thomas G. Ritch, a Mohonk "perennial," noted that the makeup of the guests, coming as they did from metropolitan areas, often was starkly opposite to the attitudes and philosophy found at Mohonk. Discussing a friend's city habits, which were cleansed by a stay at Mohonk, Mr. Ritch notes, "He might have lived longer if he had spent less time in New York and more at Mohonk." He also observed that so many city dwellers were attracted to Mohonk because of "quiet and freedom," "a change from city odors to ferns, roses and pines."

Lyman Abbott, renowned Congregational clergyman and editor, wrote a delightful account of skepticism often encountered about the Mohonk operation. The story took place in Redlands, California, when the Smileys wintered there.

Tourist: "What a beautiful place. Who does it belong to?" Driver: "A.K. Smiley." Tourist: "It must have cost a lot. How did he make his money?" Driver: "By a queer kind of hotel in New York." Tourist: "What kind of hotel?" Driver: "Well, he didn't have a bar or allow any wine to be served on the table; they didn't allow card playing, or dancing in the parlor; guests were not received nor taken away on Sunday; they have family prayers in the parlor every morning and church services on Sunday." Tourist: "Where in hell can they get patrons for such a hotel?" Driver: "They don't get their patrons from that region." ❧

Activities at Mohonk

Mohonk's vast and varied topography provided numerous opportunities for sports and athletic activities. Guests were encouraged to participate in individual and group diversions.

Golf

Built in 1903, Mohonk's golf clubhouse was one of the earliest in America.

The golf course was laid out in 1897 on the site of an existing orchard at the Mountain Rest Dairy farm. Farm and golf course coexisted for a number of years, with fruit harvesters and caddies working around each other.

Photo: Donald E. Richardson

Lantern putting tournaments were offered on midsummer evenings to the delight of putting enthusiasts.

The Putting Green was a center of social interaction and light athletics. With stalwart fans cheering the competitors, vicious weekly tournaments throughout the season culminated in the award of the coveted Mohonk Putting Trophy Cup. Genteel cutthroats were known to spy on the competition and sabotage each other's games— often requesting seats in the dining room overlooking the putting green.

PUTTING GREEN AND PORTE COCHERE, MOHONK LAKE, N. Y.

Hiking

The development of the terrain at Mohonk was focused on walking and carriage excursions. This unique blending of constructed and natural landscape resulted in the only resort of its kind, where eighty-five miles of hiking trails begin right outside the doors within a 40,000-acre natural area.

Through Mohonk's history, hiking and walking have been offered as both informal and formal activities. Founder Albert Smiley often led guests on walks through the property, and guided walks have been listed on nearly every activity schedule published. In 1933 Mohonk's first Theme Program was developed with the creation of the Shongum Outing Club weekends—now known as Hikers' Holiday.

Visitors are often struck by the uniqueness of Mohonk's outdoor offerings. In her 1971 article in *The New York Times*, Ada Louise Huxtable wrote: "The Smileys are Quakers and there is no bar, no smoking in the dining room, and you will please not play the piano in the lounge between two and five P.M. There

Albert Smiley leading guests on a walk to Gate of the Winds, 1890s.

Guests ascending a cliff, 1934.

are nature walks and bird talks and 110 miles of carefully laid out roads and trails rimming the lake and threading the woods, with 150 thatched summer-houses or gazebos along them framing stunning views, with easy spans for the geriatric. Those walks and views are fascinating for the student of 19th century landscape art. Many were laid out in the 1870s, 80s and 90s, and there is no fudging what the Victorians really admired. They wanted the 'sublime' and the 'picturesque' and at Mohonk they got it."

Hikers, early 1900s.

Lake Activities

The lake has always been central to the guest experience at Mohonk. There are many vintage pictures and stories of guests having fun in the lake—diving, swimming and other water sports—recreationally and competitively.

Historically, as today, those who preferred not to don a bathing suit could still have fun on the lake.

Rowboats were used for navigating around the lake, fishing, reading, romancing, and racing.

Francis Smiley fly-fishing, 1932.

Bathing beach, 1890s.

In the early days, a popular event for participants and spectators was the annual regatta, a rowboat race first held in August 1890. The regatta also included swimming races.

Mabel Smiley recalled that when she was a young guest at Mohonk in the 1890s, "The boats were heavy flat-bottom affairs. I know because I won my first boat race rowing with—not then, but later—my Albert, with Francis as coxswain. We observed a strict diet—roast beef every day—and went to bed early for two weeks

Mabel Smiley, regatta winner. *Left:* Regatta, 1936.

in advance of Regatta Day." Mabel also recalled "And to think of ordering an extra steak—cutting it in squares and feeding it to the fish off the office porch. Good steak, too—imagine that! ... Even though we fed steak to the fish, Mohonk had cold suppers on Sunday night, giving the cooks a night off. The horses also had a day of rest as there were no arrivals nor departures on Sunday, and no Sunday papers until the First World War."

Throughout the seasons, guests can be seen in the lake area—walking on the various routes around the

Boat House Mohonk, oil painting, Carl Werntz (1874–1944).

lake, above the lake, and beyond, sitting on the benches and in summerhouse gazebos admiring the views of the lake, and sometimes sketching, painting, and photographing the scenery.

The summerhouses and the vast porches and private balconies of the Mountain House provide multiple opportunities for viewing the lake activities, competitions, and entertainments taking place on the boat dock and surrounding areas.

Smiley family spectators (standing), Hugh, Albert, Effie, Daniel, c. 1905.

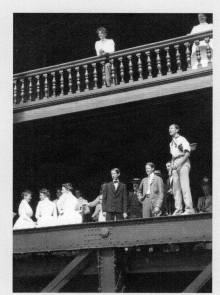

Guest spectators on the porch observing competitions.

Ice-skating

Ice-skating became a favorite lake activity when the Mountain House opened for guests during the winter months for the first time. For many decades in the mid-1900s, as winter guest patronage increased, areas of the lake near the House were cleared for ice-skating. During busier times, skating music was broadcast from the Lake Lounge porch. Strauss waltzes were a particularly popular choice.

Photo: Albert K. Smiley, II

Siblings Keith and Anna Smiley, 1935.

8

Generosity and Philanthropy

"Our guests are our friends."

Albert K. Smiley, Testimonial Gateway dedication, 1907

The construction of the Testimonial Gateway was inspired by guests wishing to honor Mohonk Mountain House founders Albert and Eliza Smiley on the occasion of their fiftieth wedding anniversary. Guests developed a special feeling of kinship with the Smiley family as they came to Mohonk for lengthy stays year after year, and 1,200 of these friends contributed funds to the erection of the gateway. Albert Smiley had chosen the architect James E. Ware a few years earlier to design the Mountain House's parlor wing, tall stone building sections, and stone porte-cochere entrances. Thus Ware was the obvious choice for this new landmark structure.

The gateway was constructed on a rise of ground about one mile from New Paltz, at the eastern edge of the Mohonk estate. Guests traveling to Mohonk were greeted by a gatekeeper who lived in the tower and, as carriages passed through the stone archway, passengers were treated to a sweeping view of the entire Shawangunk ridge including the Sky Top tower promontory. From the gateway, this new route proceeded through Mohonk farm fields and then continued through scenic woodlands ascending the steep ridge to the Mountain House.

Mohonk Lake on Monday, July 8, 1907, was the scene of a celebration honoring Albert and Eliza on their golden anniversary. The groundbreaking ceremonies took place in the morning, and several addresses were delivered by Smiley friends dealing with events and remembrances of the Smileys' life together. In the evening a celebration was held in the Mohonk Parlor, where formal plans for the gateway construction were presented. John Crosby Brown, a long-time friend of Albert and Eliza, observed in his opening remarks that he had never "acted as treasurer for an object more worthy of recognition than the cause that brings us together tonight ... and contributions came fluttering to my treasury."

Architect James E. Ware's watercolor rendering of his design for Mohonk's Testimonial Gateway, which marked the entrance road to Mohonk.

Testimonial Gateway, early 1900s.

Below: Groundbreaking ceremony, 1907.

Judge George G. Perkins, secretary of the committee, took his turn addressing the meeting and humorously described the various suggestions originally offered to honor the Smileys. Some people, he explained, wanted books with notes and a compilation of photographs of Smiley friends and admirers; others thought a great tower appropriate; while still others preferred oil portraits. "A few went to the length of promising a statue of Mr. Smiley for the garden," commented Perkins. Noting that men of distinction found that personal statues add to the terror of approaching death, he added, "Yet some

Above the gateway's arched entrance, a plaque honors Albert Keith Smiley and Eliza Phelps Smiley, the founders of Mohonk. The Latin translates as "To seek their monument, look about."

of us wanted to doom this kindly man to daily embarrassment of meeting himself, face to face, in solemn bronze or marble as he went among his flowers." Perkins concluded by declaring that, when someone suggested a gateway, "everyone seemed to be pleased with the suggestion … ." The cost estimate was $20,000, and subscriptions were to be $10 apiece.

"The major obstacles we have met with have been Mr. and Mrs. Smiley," added Perkins, "but we have gone resolutely forward ... not deterred by those we are seeking to honor." Albert Smiley accepted the tributes with characteristic modesty. "Words utterly fail me to express to you, my dear friends, my deep appreciation … ." He proceeded to name the "four red letter days" of his life. The first he said was the study of Latin

with Alfred in preparation for college. The second was the first time he met his wife-to-be, Eliza Phelps Cornell. The third day, Smiley suggested, was the discovery of Mohonk and his later purchase of it. He finished by saying, "You all must know that the fourth day is today."

On October 14, 1908, a year after the groundbreaking ceremonies, J. Edward Simmons, chairman of the Gateway Committee and president of the New York Chamber of Commerce, opened the dedication exercises for the completed Testimonial Gateway. Messages poured in from all over the nation, and many were read to the assembled crowd of well-wishers. A final tally of 1,300 subscriptions totaled about $20,000—over $500,000 in today's dollars. Albert Smiley responded to the formal presentation by declaring, "You could not possibly have made us any gift that would have given us more intense pleasure than this gateway. You should have seen me drive down five miles every two or three days this summer," he related, "and each time climb up steep ladders, under protest from my family, till finally the topmost story was reached, watching with all the enthusiasm of a boy the huge boulders, weighing many tons each, lifted by steam power and carefully placed in position by skillful masons."

Smiley also related his future plans to lay macadam roads and plant trees and shrubbery around the tower. "We have growing in our nursery house two thousand trees and shrubs ready for planting and are negotiating for more."

In responding to the gift of the gateway, Albert Smiley captured the essence of his hopes for Mohonk and spoke simply but eloquently of its future:

It is most desirable that it should always prove a success as heretofore in its management. Ardently do I desire that a large share of the profits arising from a wise administration of this estate may be used for the good of mankind. I feel sure that the remarkable natural beauty of this large domain will continue to be developed on artistic lines for many ages to come.

In the sunset of life it is an unspeakable gratification that we have a younger brother and his wife who with their children are all interested in maintaining a Christian home where just dealing will prevail, where warm greetings will be extended and kindly interest shown to all. It is a still greater pleasure to feel that for generations to come streams of high-minded, distinguished philanthropists will pass through the portals of this gateway every spring and autumn to discuss great national and international questions which will help to solve some of the great problems of society, and make Mohonk a veritable delectable mountain, known in the remotest corners of the world for its high aims and warm interest in every movement for the betterment of mankind.

Booker T. Washington and Mohonk

Causes of social justice were important to the members of Smiley's Quaker family, and he continually looked for ways to leverage Mohonk Mountain House to help those that he could. In addition to tireless work for Native Americans through service on the Board of Indian Commissioners and the Mohonk Conferences, Smiley also looked to assist African Americans in the decades following the Civil War and to end the legal enslavement of other human beings. "You have been so true and real a friend of the man of color … ," wrote African American musician Harry T. Burleigh to Albert K. Smiley in 1901.

As a lifelong educator, Smiley knew well the importance of education and its benefit to peoples seeking to better themselves. Through friendships, public service, hotel guests, and the many Mohonk conferences, the Smileys were part of an impressive constellation of reformers, policy makers, and philanthropists. Through these relationships they became friends with leaders of the day, including Hollis B. Frissell from Hampton Institute in Virginia, whose school served both African Americans and Native Americans, and Booker T. Washington, an alumnus of Hampton and founder of Tuskegee Institute in Alabama. Smiley saw the opportunity that came in the form of a captive audience at Mohonk House,

Booker T. Washington—glass slide, c. 1900. Glass slides were used in lantern slide presentations in the Mohonk Parlor.

and brought leaders of important causes to present their work to the guests.

Both Hampton and Tuskegee were among those invited to make presentations at Mohonk annually during the late nineteenth and early twentieth century. In addition to a lecture about the work of the represented cause, entertainment was also provided. For several years Hampton brought a musical quartet of students, and Harry Burleigh often accompanied Booker T. Washington for the Tuskegee presentation, singing both classical and spiritual selections.

Local resident Guy Davenport wrote in his reminiscences of the early 1900s when he was employed at Mohonk:

> Through these conferences, Booker T. Washington, the President of Tuskegee College for negroes in Alabama, came to Mohonk for several days each season I was here. He was always accompanied by a small group of Negro students in the interest of raising money to carry on and enlarge on the work he was doing at Tuskegee. The main parlor was reserved one evening of each of his visits for Booker T.'s talk and singing by the male students. Booker T. was one of the most eloquent speakers I have ever listened to, and the students were excellent singers. He was doing wonderful work at Tuskegee, training the younger Negros as farmers, teachers, homemakers, and in various trades.
>
> The Parlor was usually filled to standing room to hear his talk and the singing. It was customary to take up a collection at the close of his talk. Mr. Smiley started this with his check for $1000. Several other guests were reported to give equal amounts, and other guests were very generous, too.

Willis S. Martin, working as a telephone operator 1912–1913, recalled:

> Dr. Washington's talk dealt with the situation among Negroes and outlined a most viable future for them, based on their contribution to society through work and the assurance of financial compensation would most surely follow. … Mr. A.K. [Smiley] always had a small table in the Parlor near the speaker on which he placed an old high-crown straw hat to receive donations from the audience. As I recall, the hat was well filled and I'm sure that Tuskegee profited substantially from the talk by Dr. Washington. The following morning I handled some telegrams for Dr. Washington and talked with him.

The famous Albert Smiley hat, passed around audiences or left on a table
for Mountain House guests to contribute money for a good cause.

Mohonkers felt impelled to give of themselves and their means to support worthy causes
they learned about at Mohonk. In 1894, just one year after a major financial recession in the
United States, Mohonkers donated $519 to Tuskegee, more than $14,000 in today's dollars.
Two years later, guests gave Tuskegee $1,200, or $33,000 in today's dollars. Guests were generous, indeed. Some who spent multiple seasons at Mohonk became as invested in the causes
presented as the Smileys were. In 1905 one guest spent the summer at the beach instead of
at Mohonk, but wrote to Albert Smiley, "As my contributions to Tuskegee, Hampton & Mrs.
Booth's work have been made principally through Mohonk, I enclose my check … ."

As one might imagine, the Smileys became inundated by worthy causes interested in pre-
senting their work. Sometimes guests made donations to benefit that cause. In response to
one such request in 1908, Smiley replied, "I have found that there is a sentiment among the
guests of the house to the effect that they are being called upon [to make contributions] too
frequently… ." It became necessary to become selective.

Redlands, California

It may not seem relevant at first blush to the story of Mohonk, but Albert Smiley's philanthropies ranged from coast to coast. Close friends even remarked, "The Smileys made their money at Mohonk and spent it in California." A winter residence in Redlands, California, demanded time, energy, and expense. The gift of a downtown park and library in Redlands, as well as service as a trustee of Pomona College, Brown University, and New Paltz Normal School, required considerable resources. Albert Smiley was not afraid to borrow to see his benefactions enacted, however, because Daniel was there to back his efforts and somehow generate the funds out of the Mohonk operation.

The 200-acre property known as Cañon Crest Park, or popularly called "Smiley Heights"—Albert Smiley's winter residence in the hills overlooking Redlands, California—was their private residence and landscaped arboretum. The arboretum was kept open for many years for the enjoyment of the public as a tourist attraction. At a later time, a change in tax policy by the City of Redlands forced the family to close this beautiful park, until then maintained by them as a benefit to the community.

President Theodore Roosevelt, traveling through the country on a political campaign, visited Albert Smiley at the winter home in Cañon Crest Park on May 7, 1903. When Roosevelt arrived at the Southern Pacific station in Redlands, the whole town turned out "in gala dress" to greet him. He was entertained by the governor of California and given the grand tour. The president was "in admiration of the beauties of Redlands," adding "it would be impossible to imagine anything more delightful … ."

It was largely through Roosevelt's connection with Albert Smiley's Mohonk conferences and Albert's membership on the United States Board of Indian Commissioners that the president's first stop in California was Redlands. According to the local newspapers, Cañon Crest Park was the only private residence he visited. Upon learning of Roosevelt's trip to Redlands, Harrison Gray Otis, publisher of the *Los Angeles Times*, allegedly grumbled, "How in hell did Redlands get him before Los Angeles?"

The use of funds from Mohonk to support these projects and properties caused Daniel much administrative effort and not a little worry. He wholeheartedly supported his brother's indefatigable impulses for service, however, and even added to his own burdens by serving on the Board of Trustees of Vassar College, his alma mater Haverford College, and the University of Redlands, as well as on the United States Board of Indian Commissioners. ❧

343 PRESIDENT ROOSEVELT AT REDLANDS MAY 7 1903

President Theodore Roosevelt in his carriage, being greeted by Albert K. Smiley (with his back to the camera).

Old Boys

By the turn of the twentieth century, an informal group that centered around Albert K. Smiley became known as "the Old Boys Club." It included Mountain House guests prominent in legal and State Supreme Court circles, noted clergy, a former governor of New York, and businessmen connected to New York City cultural life. They golfed, enjoyed fireworks, and gently poked fun at each other with humorous banter. They were a key factor in raising funds and planning for the Testimonial Gateway presented in 1908 to honor Albert and Eliza's fiftieth wedding anniversary.

"Old Boys" (seated left to right) Theodore Cuyler, Albert K. Smiley, Judge Goodrich, (standing left to right) Thomas J. Yorke, Judge Perkins, Gov. Benjamin Odell, John V. Craven, Thomas Marshall, Col. Walter Franklin, c. 1905.

At the dedication of the Mohonk Spring in 1904, they took every opportunity to lampoon each other's affinity for either water or whiskey. Calling the ceremony to order, Albert referred to the event as "an Old Boys" celebration. "I have nothing to do with it," he noted, but "these old boys cannot be resisted any more than old girls can." Observing that the spring provided pure, drinkable water, Smiley told of the "great deal of work" required to cut through ten feet of rock and to landscape the area.

The Revered Theodore Cuyler declared, "Nature is always a total abstainer … It is a prohibitionist."

Judge George Perkins, when it was his time at the podium, stated that it was "incongruous" to call on "a man from Kentucky to speak at this dedica-tion of a water spring." He argued that a Kentuckian would see the spring and lake and exclaim, "water, water, everywhere, but not a drop to drink." He added that "more liquor is drunk in New England than in Kentucky … [but] I am unwilling to admit that a New Englander can outstrip a Kentuckian in anything."

Albert Smiley's father-in-law, John V. Craven, provided the final remarks, recalling coming to Mohonk in early years and how he had seen it evolve. Nothing surprised him more than, two years before, being called up to receive a punch bowl as a ten-nis prize. "Mohonk was the last place I would have expected to find a punch bowl." "It was an appropri-ate gift," Albert chimed in, to much laughter.

Dedication of the Mohonk Spring, 1904.

9

Changes and Challenges

"I am particularly anxious that as a family we shall all pull together harmoniously. We have strong wills and divided opinion by inheritance."

Daniel Smiley, 1911, Family Conference

The turn of the century brought awareness that the younger Smiley family members were being primed to fill the shoes of Albert, who was now in his early seventies.

On December 2, 1912, Albert Smiley died peacefully at his winter home in Redlands, California. Eighty-four years of life closed amid success and achievement. It is ironic that, unknown to Albert, a group of leading American citizens led by former secretaries of state John W. Foster and Elihu Root had placed his name in nomination for the Nobel Peace Prize. Everyone connected with the plan felt sure that Albert Smiley would have received the 1913 Prize had he lived, but the Nobel Committee did not at that time award prizes posthumously.

People's relations to people and to nature had become the underpinning of the Mohonk operation. A clientele of sympathetic persons possessed of varied backgrounds constituted Mohonk's guests. A unique experience in fashioning a harmony between wilderness and the arts of humankind continued to broaden its outreach. Concern for improving

Bert, Daniel, Ruth, Eliza, Effie, Albert, Francis, and Hugh Smiley, c. 1900.

the world began to assume different manifestations.

Yet it was not easy. Money was made abundantly, but it was spent abundantly upon house improvements, new roads, new summerhouses, increased conference activities, and nationwide charitable causes.

Still, loans needed to be paid, obligations met, and Mohonk's responsibilities to guests and employees alike maintained. To the members of his family, Daniel Smiley turned for support. "I suggest that our motto for the family be the one word 'Together,'" he told them. He urged them individually and collectively to "live up to its full meaning."

Daniel's wife Effie's guidance, sage advice, soothing manners, and ability to deal with vagaries of human nature made her role a key factor in Mohonk's development between 1912 and 1951. She served as hostess, owing to the semi-invalid state of Eliza Smiley, and brought to that role grace and assurance. Effie shared with her husband a sense of stewardship over Mohonk. Not "mine" but "ours" became the attitude in expressing the Mohonk responsibilities.

The early 1900s had seen a fast pace in physical improvements to the Mountain House, and new roads as well. In 1901 Bonticou Road was extended and the present power plant built. In 1903 Undercliff Road was created along a talus slope; also built were Terrace Drive, the golf clubhouse at Mountain Rest, and the Artists Lodge. In 1904 Bonticou Road was again extended, and North Lookout Road was carved out. In 1907 Picnic Lodge opened, and Minnewaska Road was completed. Between 1908 and 1913, a third stage road to New Paltz was built, the dining room circle extension was completed, new tennis courts were added, the golf course was lengthened and improved, a croquet court was laid out, and the

Francis, Daniel, Ruth, Effie, Bert, Eliza, Hugh, and Albert Smiley, in a carefully posed photograph, 1904.

first issue of the *Lake Mohonk Weekly Bulletin* (May 1912) appeared. In order to encourage supervisors and heads of departments to live with their families on the mountain, a small colony of houses called Cottage Grove was constructed.

Daniel and Effie Smiley's three sons—A.K. Smiley, Jr. (named for his uncle), Hugh, and Francis G.—assisted in the management of the hotel. Hugh

Francis Smiley.

ca 1923

Effie and Daniel Smiley, 1923.

became the first editor of the *Bulletin*. His wife, Hester, was involved in social and entertainment duties, the gift shop, and furnishing the guest rooms and public spaces. In the early 1920s Hugh left the family business to start his own resort operation in Massachusetts, and while his tenure at Mohonk was comparatively brief, his kindliness with guests, his design of the Laurels residence, and his appreciation for Mohonk's tradition helped his father considerably.

Daniel and Effie's daughter Ruth became increasingly involved with Mohonk duties during the 1900s. She was the sports director, helped with the Picnic Lodge operation, and frequently accompanied her father as he made his rounds about the property. Ruth later moved to California and was married there, settling on the Redlands property with her family.

A.K. Smiley, Jr., or "Bert" as he was known to close friends and family, and Francis ("Doc") became their father's able assistants. Bert Smiley took naturally to the operations end of the family business, while Francis took delight in overseeing the Mohonk farms, engineering matters, and outside improvements, as well as accounting procedures.

One of the strengths of the Smiley family was the fact that spouses not only served as loving life partners, but also lent quality, creativity, and fresh ideas to the Mohonk operation. Bert married Mabel A. Craven, daughter of Mohonk guests and close family friends John V. and Anna Craven of Pennsylvania. Mr. Craven was a man of wide business experience

Bert Smiley, 1929.

Francis and Bert Smiley, 1945.

Photo: P. Hodges Boublier

and an appreciator of Mohonk's two-fold outreach toward people and nature. Mabel was instrumental in the management of the housekeeping department and advised on matters of employee relations.

Frank Craven, a brother of Mabel, was associated with Mohonk for a brief period during the time when Mohonk was first developing a fleet of autos and trucks. He was the first to operate the Mountain Rest transfer when guests came in cars, and during the winters served as Mohonk postmaster. He was a beloved friend of many members of the family and staff.

Francis Smiley was no less fortunate in meeting and marrying his wife. In 1915 the Arbitration Conference delegates subscribed funds to purchase a choralcelo, one of the latest innovations in the musical world, a blend of the piano and organ. In 1919 a lovely instrumentalist came to play the choralcelo, Rachel Orcutt from Boston. The mountain was to become her home, for she and Francis were married in 1920. With grace, kindness, and talent as a performer, Rachel added her abilities to the Mountain House's cultural endeavors. ✍

Mabel and Bert Smiley, 1945.
At right: Francis Smiley, seated by Rachel Smiley playing the choralcelo.

10

Mohonk's Golden Anniversary

*"With great earnestness of purpose, but in all humility,
I accept the heritage."*

Daniel Smiley

The sincerity with which Daniel Smiley assumed ownership of Mohonk was real indeed, but so were the challenges confronting him, which threatened to impede and even curtail certain aspects of Mohonk goals.

The shot at Sarajevo in 1914 proved to be a fire bell in the night. Three years later America entered World War I, "the war to end all wars." War was personally objectionable to the Smiley Quaker conscience, and the direct effect of it upon Mohonk brought an end to the conferences and produced shock waves upon the business.

Both the Indian and arbitration conferences were cancelled for 1917—a decision thought to be temporary, but from which the two enterprises never recovered. Faced with substantial debts, the result of Albert's philanthropies and the tide of war, which had thrown the nation into social upheaval, Daniel Smiley and his sons had all they could do to keep the Mountain House secure.

The years of World War I and those that followed brought about startling social changes in America. As a creation of a nineteenth-century ethos, Mohonk faced the challenge of survival. In its formative years it was a resort for people of reputation, means, and philanthropic influence. Its appointments were the most modern available at the time. The clientele read as from a chapter on American business and social history, ranging from John Arbuckle, the coffee merchant, to John D. Rockefeller, the oil magnate, and from Mrs. Ulysses S. Grant to philanthropist Helen M. Gould. Edward Everett Hale came to Mohonk to write in peace, and John Burroughs came to savor and interpret the wonders of nature. But most of them had passed, and a new order took their place.

Daniel became increasingly aware that Mohonk's future depended on finding a balance between maintaining its guiding principles while enabling its business model to embrace the changing world and the shifted expectations of Mohonk guests. His concern is expressed in his memorandum of November 2, 1917, "Mohonk Ideals":

> Reminded by some changes this year necessarily taking place in our working staff and by repeated demands for "improvement" in certain details of administration and equipment, I have been giving much time during the past few weeks to considering the traditions and ideals of this House.
>
> In reviewing the methods which have built up this business, I find most predominant not material matters. They have been helpful, but it is not excellence in equipment or service which have made our reputation and laid the solid foundation of present success. It is rather, in spite of deficiencies in almost every material direction, that the business has grown and a most enviable reputation acquired.
>
> It is absolutely certain that the attraction which has brought together here a houseful of the very best people in our country and induced them to return year after year was not an excellent table nor superior service; it was not commodious apartments nor expensive furnishings; it was not constant attentions from a numerous and highly-paid office staff nor a long retinue of bell boys, door men and porters; it was not swell carriages for driving nor uniforms and brass buttons nor an abundance of servants nor the sophistication of the few then here; it was not high-sounding names for positions and for those who filled them, copied from ultra-fashionable city hotels; it was none of the pomp and circumstance of the fashionable watering places.
>
> The conditions under which this business developed were those pertaining to the everyday life of the farmer, the school teacher and the Quaker. They were simplicity, thoroughness and hominess.
>
> The forces which built up and have all along maintained this business were scen-

ery, wholesome mental and moral atmosphere, plain living, fair business methods. Later changes in the direction of more luxurious living have added something to our reputation, but have involved expense overhead for which no adequate return is received.

A month later, he added:

… the reputation of this House was early made when there was hardly a decent sleeping or public room in the building; when the variety of food was limited and no hot dishes served for supper; the grounds were shabby; the stables close to the door; the carriages clumsy and mean; there was no service of bell boys and no electric bells; tallow candles were the only light in sleeping rooms; and there wasn't a private bath in the house. Sleeping rooms were carpeted with China matting; halls with coarse cocoa matting and the parlor with ingrain [fiber dyed before weaving] carpet; but guests met a spirit of hospitality and kindness which offset the lack of comforts and luxuries so that they remained content.

My idea in bringing this to mind now is for a reminder that we must not be carried away with the idea that there is a need for a country summer resort to provide the equipments in fittings, furnishings, food or service of a city hotel. It is rather with simplicity, hominess, courtesy and kind personal attention that we will win out. The putting on of show and style will do us harm.

The recession of 1919 caused further concern about Mohonk's survival, but the overall situation eased somewhat by 1920. Through prudent planning, careful budgeting, and personal physical strain, Daniel Smiley pulled Mohonk out of debt and kept a faithful clientele. He even sent funds to A.K. Smiley Public Library near the Smiley's winter home in Redlands, California, for a children's wing. Despite the struggles of the post-war recovery, Mohonk's fiftieth anniversary was celebrated with fanfare on June 1, 1920. The speeches given to commemorate this golden anniversary reflected both pride and admiration for the success of Mohonk's first fifty years, which Daniel Smiley summarized at the start of celebration:

The business has steadily prospered. The 300 acres have increased to 5,600. The little house has spread out to a length of 700 feet, with a considerable number of subordinate buildings in some of which very considerable industries are carried on, contributing to the main business. Flower gardens and lawns have grown where there was at the beginning merely a confusion of rocks and stumps and dwarf trees. From some twenty acres of fruit trees and vegetables, the farms have increased to 1,500 acres. Sixty miles of private roads have been constructed, with paths and summerhouses and seats, and the number of guests who can be accommodated now considerably exceeds four hundred.

The idea my brother Albert had in purchasing this place was to make a summer home for himself and his family and his friends. He found that the income of a rather successful school teacher was not sufficient to develop the place according to his visions, and it became a summer resort in addition to a family home.

The accumulation of money for its own sake has never appealed to our family as a worthy occupation. In a very real sense we do not look on ourselves as irresponsible owners, but as trustees or stewards with the mandate of administering the property for the recreation and enjoyment of visitors equally with ourselves.

The keynote speaker for the evening celebration event was Rev. Dr. Samuel J. Fisher, an old-time Mohonker and nationally known Presbyterian clergyman. Excerpts appeared in an ensuing *Mohonk Bulletin*:

Is it not rare that the history of any hotel, however splendid or spacious or famous, calls for special mention after fifty years? Usually, however associated with men or incidents, with great social functions or politics, its life or ending is of no marked importance.

But we cannot so regard Mohonk because it has been more than an inn, more than a hotel. It has had characteristics that set it apart from other hostelries and invest it with a singular interest, strangely pleasing and permanent.

Most hotels owe their origin and attraction to the commercial instincts and financial genius of their builder. But Mohonk was the product of Mr. Albert K. Smiley's character and intellect, as well as of his executive ability. He wove himself into it. He molded it so that everywhere the pressure of his hand is seen.

In planning for the fiftieth anniversary, Mohonk commissioned an artwork to commemorate the special landmark year. The image graced the cover of the annual brochure and other publications. The artwork

Mohonk's fiftieth-anniversary brochure, 1921.

still hangs in the Mountain House. Unfortunately, the identity of the artist remains a mystery.

As Mohonk endeavored to overcome the difficulties inherent in wartime America, the planning of projects and new activities went forward, including upgrades to the power plant.

The problems posed by the post–World War I era might well have written Mohonk's last chapter, as happened to other resorts of an era now irrevocably lost. By clinging to a brilliant past and failing to adapt to an uncertain future, other resort hotels had lost their appeal and their chance of survival. The prudent planning of Daniel Smiley and the unified efforts of his family created an atmosphere where Mohonk used its past as a basis for attraction and not merely as a reflection of past history. New approaches were designed for the Mohonk experience, where guests could be challenged and stimulated to use all their faculties in helping to discover the new needs of society and to search for timeless values through contact with nature.

Seeking to leave a legacy structure to honor founder Albert K. Smiley upon Mohonk's fiftieth anniversary, guests and family focused on a landmark tower for Sky Top. ◆

Photo: Albert K. Smiley, II

In 1917 a new kind of steam boiler was proudly delivered by six white horses. The last of the wood-burning Franklin stoves was removed, and radiators were finally installed throughout the House. The new boiler enabled a more efficient system for supplying steam for cooking and for heating the Mountain House rooms.

The Story of the Sky Top Towers

The Albert K. Smiley Memorial Tower has stood on Mohonk's iconic escarpment since 1923. The tower was constructed from quartz conglomerate rock (known locally as "Shongum Grit") that was quarried at its base. The digging and blasting began in 1921, and the quarry hole became the Sky Top reservoir. This is the fourth in a series of towers at Sky Top, the previous ones having been destroyed by wind or fire.

First Tower, 1870

In January 1870, before the Mountain House opened its doors for the first guests, Alfred Smiley initiated plans for the first tower to be constructed on Sky Top, a promontory that had long awarded hikers with magnificent views of the surrounding valleys and distant mountains. The wooden tower was octagonal and measured 8 ¾ feet in diameter and 20 feet tall—high enough for observers to see the Mountain House over the trees. Three chains tethered the tower to nearby tree trunks to provide stability, but unfortunately the tower was toppled by high winds after only one month.

Second Tower, 1872–1877

Two years later, the next tower was created. Alfred Smiley sent his brother Albert a sketch in March 1872 detailing the proposed structure: the outside was to be built of "4 ½ inch matched pine nearly free from knots"; it was to have three stories with an open plat-

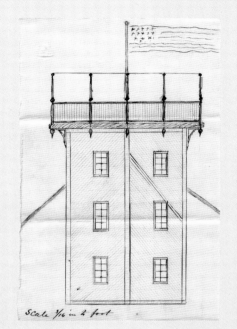

Scale 1/16 in 2 foot

Alfred's sketch of the second tower.

Below: The completed tower replicated the sketch quite accurately.

form on top; and, importantly, the plans included heavy guy wires to steady the tower during storms. However, fire, not wind, caused its demise five years later, in 1877.

Third Tower, 1878–1909

Undaunted by the destructive forces of nature, in the spring of 1878 Alfred Smiley made plans to construct a third tower. The original concept included a tower with four floors, four platforms, and seven flights of stairs. But, Albert was in a hurry to have the tower completed

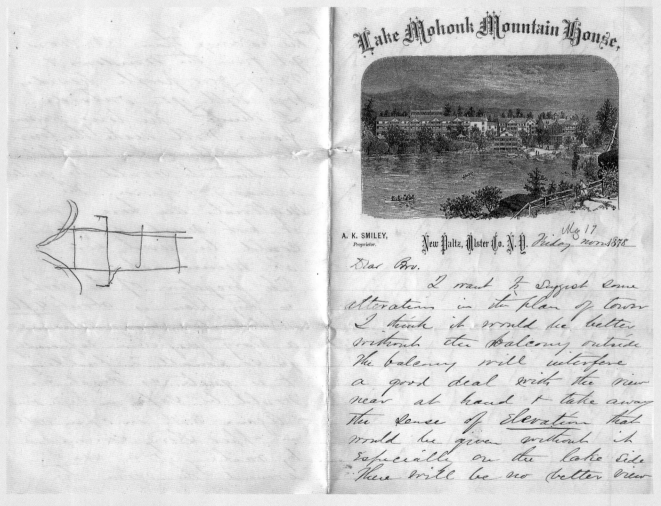

Alfred's sketch of the third tower.

The completed third tower.

Photo: J. Loeffler

before the summer season, so Alfred sent a rudimentary sketch to his brother suggesting a less elaborate plan with just one observation platform. The third tower managed to survive for thirty-one years before burning to the ground in 1909.

Fourth Tower, 1923–Present

In 1919, New York State proposed building a steel tower on Sky Top for use as a forest fire lookout station. There was strong resistance to this idea from both Mohonk guests and the Smiley family. At the time of Mohonk's fiftieth anniversary the following year, a committee of guests was formed to plan an attractive memorial tower to Albert K. Smiley. The committee contacted Allen and Collins, architects from Boston known for their Gothic revival buildings. The lead architect, Francis F. Allen, not only offered several design renderings for the committee to peruse, but donated his services for the project. Nearly one hundred guests contributed funds for the tower's construction.

Building the tower required intense labor: highly-skilled local stone masons cut, shaped, and carefully placed each stone in the structure; workers operated

The fourth tower took two years to complete, from 1921–1923.

the portable steam-powered drill; others handled the horses and the derrick used for hoisting large rock chunks; a blacksmith was on site to sharpen bits and hand tools; and a stone cutter was on hand for the finish work on the stone surfaces.

The cupola being delivered.

11

Daniel Smiley,
Mohonk's Squire

"I suggest that our motto for the family be the one word 'together' and that individually and collectively we live up to its full meaning."

Daniel Smiley

The construction of the Albert K. Smiley Memorial Tower at Sky Top and the subsequent dedication exercises seemed a reaffirmation of Mohonk's purpose—its commitment to a quality resort experience as well as to the social goals maintained by the Smiley family. Daniel Smiley, with a propensity for organization and a management team including sons Albert (Bert) and Francis, served Mohonk well during the decade of the 1920s.

Reviewing briefly Daniel's role in the operation of Mohonk permits a better understanding of the atmosphere that Bert and Francis enjoyed as youths for empirical training in hotel management. It was indeed a baptism by experience. In 1881 Daniel took an active role in the management of the property. He ultimately planned the entire Mountain House, save the section built in 1879 before his arrival. Nearly all the roads came under his "engineering eye," and the development of forestry and the extensive Mohonk farm operation were his. Daniel, even though not trained as an engineer, through acquired knowledge supervised the planning of the civil, electrical, and mechanical engineering projects demanded by Mohonk's growth.

Just as Daniel had done for them, Francis and Bert trained their children in the varied facets of the Mohonk business from the ground up. A typical set of experiences is expressed by Bert's son, Keith Smiley, about the work that he and his brother Dan undertook:

> … the first job was painting signs; another activity we did through the same years was an unusual type of job and rather fascinating to us … somewhat like a treasure hunt. We were assigned periodically to comb the immediate area around the Mountain House for any sort of receptacle that might be a place where stagnant water could collect and breed mosquitoes, because before the days of all the sprays this was a practical way of getting rid of mosquito-breeding possibilities that might bother the guests. Also, we had traps for flies around the kitchen and dining rooms. Things of this sort were all special assignments.

While Daniel was necessarily quite conscious of the strain of operating an efficient and gracious hotel, his guests were never aware of the problems he encountered. To keep a balance in life, he devoted much time to landscape gardening and the development of a subtle blend between natural scenery and the need to alter some of the natural environment to serve recreational purposes. As a result of these interests, he assembled an extensive and rare library on landscape gardening, forestry, and related subjects. This splendid collection guided the visual beauties of Mohonk, which many visitors and guests credited to nature alone.

Effie Smiley, complementing her husband's interests, took over supervision of the flower gardens and the cultivated grounds around the Mountain House. As mistress of Mohonk she served as the gracious hostess of numerous conferences and meetings and extended the kind word or helpful suggestion to guests. Her influence behind the scenes was appreciated by both guests and staff, although her specific contributions often went unheralded. She, too, was a familiar figure driving her faithful horse Kerney about the Mohonk property with Borghild Fossum, her assistant and companion.

The familiar figure of Daniel Smiley astride "Sunshine," his vigorous and handsome Kentucky-trained horse with natural "white socks," became a welcome sight to guests during the 1920s as he rode about the grounds on tours of inspection. This image led some to refer to Daniel as "Mohonk's Squire."

Meanwhile, the automobile remained something of an anathema to Daniel Smiley. While Mohonk's arriving guests were met in New Paltz by a Mohonk carriage until the early 1900s, after World War I the automobile began to replace the slower-paced horse-drawn vehicles. That the interests of time may have been well served did not, for Daniel Smiley, make up for the gentle clomping of horses' hooves upon the winding shale-covered roads. The carriage possessed graciousness and rhythm in contrast to the sputtering, gravel-gnashing auto, whose only purpose in life seemed to be speed and quick access. Daniel banned automobiles from the property. He wrote reprovingly in 1929:

Automobiles are kept out because they do not contribute to quiet and restfulness. To banish from this mountain noise and dirt and disorderliness, to keep the atmosphere sweet and clear, has been, and is, a primary aim requiring vigilance and labor and expense beyond belief. For this reason, at a great additional expense, hard instead of soft coal is burned at the power house. While the presence of automobiles would offend in these particulars, a great change has taken place also during the past ten years in the sentiments of those who use cars elsewhere and even make the journey here in them. The overwhelming consensus among guests has come to be that these are disturbers of quiet, however useful elsewhere, and should continue to be banished from this reservation. With minor and obvious exceptions, it is the well-known policy here to ascertain what guests desire and then give it to them. It is perfectly clear that for the present time the great majority of guests do not wish automobiles coming up to the door, while they do almost unanimously desire roads for horseback riding and walking to be free from sudden terror at every sharp turn around projecting bluffs.

Later, in the 1930s, after Daniel's death and the onset of the Depression, a modification was made—guests' automobiles were permitted to traverse Mohonk's roads, but a pilot from the Mountain House had to do the driving. In the 1950s the policy changed to allow arriving guests to drive their own cars directly to the Mountain House. The former sense of leisurely pace continues to be maintained by asking guests to enter the property slowly, so that time is allowed for unwinding and becoming mentally prepared for the Mohonk experience; posted speed limits are twenty miles per hour, and signs admonish, "Slowly and Quietly, Please."

Because of the automobile and the new mobility it heralded, in 1925 Daniel Smiley and his sons constructed Lenape Lane in connection with an old stage road. This became the approach for cars through the Testimonial Gateway up to Mountain Rest, the entrance point to the Mohonk House and grounds.

Run by J. Irving Goddard from 1891 to 1907, Mountain Rest was originally a boardinghouse established by the Drew family. Guests at Mountain Rest could take advantage of Mountain House programs and activities while staying in these less expensive quarters. Following the boardinghouse's destruction by fire in 1907, a new Mountain Rest business began, consisting of a bungalow colony and teahouse run by Hugh and Hester Smiley. After Hugh Smiley departed from Mohonk, Irving Goddard came back to operate the Mountain Rest House and Cottages.

The 1920s saw another innovation by the Smileys. Mabel Craven Smiley wished to continue the family's concern for education. The distance to schools in nearby New Paltz became formidable in the winter for her children Daniel, Keith, and Anna, as well as for other children residing at Mohonk. In 1920 Mabel became founder and owner of the Mohonk School. It was a private school for boys, located on the Mohonk property in the Grove Building section of the Mountain House on the second, third, and fourth floors.

Mohonk provided an idyllic setting for the boarding students, offering a wide variety of outdoor activities ranging from team sports, horse-related activities, and bicycle and ski tours, to more unique activities such as cabin building and farming.

Left: Students on a sleigh ride, c. 1955.

Below: The Mountain House, closed in the winter for guests, provided facilities for the Mohonk School.

Students at
Cope's Lookout,
1937.

During the Depression, the Mountain House opened for winter business for the first time to augment Mohonk's income. The school changed to a junior school format rather than exclusively college preparatory, and the Smiley partnership took over ownership. Beginning in 1958, Mr. and Mrs. E.M. Lafferty, former principals at the Mohonk School, continued the venture as a separate entity from Mohonk. The Mohonk School moved to the Cragsmoor Inn, and later moved to a location near Wallkill, New York, before its eventual closing.

During these years, and to a large extent for the two following decades, self-sufficiency was one of the hallmarks of the Mohonk operation. Daniel and Effie had worked closely with Bert and Mabel and with Francis and Rachel. Now they had the opportunity of watching their grandchildren grow up in the Mohonk environment and take their place in Mohonk's operation.

A group of Mohonk farms provided the Mountain House with fresh milk, some fresh vegetables, and meats. Refuse from the hotel kitchen was fed to the pigs; the pig farm produced pork for the tables. Animal fats, salvaged in the kitchen, were used to manufacture a yellow soap, which in turn was used in the kitchen and laundry. The operation of the farms by 1930 saw nearly forty men employed, working with twenty horses and two tractors. Nearly 1,000 acres of Mohonk land were cultivated or in pasture. Francis Smiley took special interest in the dairy herds and the pig farm, and in keeping the extensive records on both.

Haying at Brook Farm, at the foot of the mountain, 1941.

Until 1958 Mohonk also produced its own electrical and heating power using expensive anthracite coal, which burned cleaner for energy efficiency and for low pollution. Wood served as the principal fuel used in the power plant during the Depression of the 1930s and during World War II. As was noted in *The Mohonk Bulletin* May 26, 1934, "Cordwood harvested by local men in need of employment from our own forest crop, continues to take the place of coal as fuel to produce light and heat."

Stacks of cordwood
stretched along miles
of carriage roads near
enough to the Mountain
House to be easily
transported to the Power
House. Substantial
manpower was required
to supply this form of
energy—for instance,
in 1941 the amount of
labor for wood-chopping
alone totaled 4,686
"man days."

Photo: Daniel Smiley, Jr.

Photo: Daniel Smiley, Jr.

When the House closes for guests in the autumn, immediate preparation for the next season begins. For three months in autumn and spring the housekeeper has a company ... men and women taking up, cleaning and relaying carpets, papering, painting, varnishing and renovating rooms. The man in charge of sanitation, while busy every day in the year, has his inning at all places then unoccupied. This is an important office, waging unremitting war on the whole race of undesirable germ-producing citizens, out-of-doors and within, ranging in size all the way up from the minute organism scarcely visible under a microscope, to rats and weasels and the night prowling dog in guilty quest of garbage and trouble generally. A force of plumbers, too, is busy all winter, and carpenters making repairs outside and in. There are ten to twenty painters on wagons and automobiles, which are also overhauled and repairs made. Light driving horses are put in box stalls and have yards for exercise. A part of the 2,500-ton coal supply is drawn up the mountain. The aim is to cut and draw to the power house two thousand cords of wood each winter.

The slate-crushing plant and the Shawangunk grit plant are also operated to provide a supply of surfacing material for roads, and many miles of our drives and paths are each year covered with these materials. The cutting of wood and timber is done on scientific private estate and forestry lines with a view to encouraging laurel, dogwood, azalea, rhododendron, and other flowering plants, as well as trees having beautiful autumn foliage; and there is also cutting away trees to open distant views. In the winter the greenhouses and thousands of bedding plants require attention. … There is in autumn the fertilizing of flower beds and lawns and covering tender plants with leaves and pine boughs, and in the spring the care of hotbeds and sowing of flower seed and the putting out of thousands of annuals, and planting trees in cultivated ground and woods. Keeping open roads after each snowstorm, and shoveling enormous drifts from roofs of buildings all continue. Provisions and coal and a vast variety of supplies must be drawn by horses when snow is too deep for auto truck, and ice gathered from the lake. … Watchmen go their rounds indoors and out. The laundry is operated. Hickory and rock oak, too, must be drawn to the big woodshed and sawed by power and split by hand and piled to season and be ready for the cheerful open fires.

With the help of Mabel and Bert's sons Dan and Keith, the 1930s saw a host of improvements and innovation at Mohonk. New activities began for the pleasure and involvement of guests. The first rock climbing took place on the Trapps section of the Mohonk property. Another activity begun during this period was the Mohonk Trail Riders, originated by Edward B. Jones, the house manager. The first trip began in October 1932, and the fee charged was $35 for three days. During each trip, Trail Riders rode fifty miles along ridge-top trails. The calamity of World War II ended the Mohonk Trail Riders, who last rode in 1942.

The Shongum Outing Club took its first Mohonk walk in September 1933. The members traversed many of the carriage roads and trails in rugged moun-

Ed Jones leads this trail ride in 1932, with Dan Smiley second in command. Those who accumulated 400 trail-ride miles over a sequence of visits were awarded a special studded horse collar with a brass, heart-shaped medallion on the front, and personal name plate on top. These "mileage achievers" usually rode in the lead positions on the trail rides.

tain terrain. These outings were usually three days in duration, continuing in later decades as a specific theme program for hikers.

Out of economic adversity came still other innovations and a subtle, distinct change in Mohonk's strategy. Where conferences and philanthropic outreach had been predominant prior to World War I, a new era was now at hand. The energies of the family safeguarded Mohonk's tradition and its very existence. This called for the utilization of Mohonk's

Photo: Daniel Smiley, Jr.

These ladies, posing in 1936, more proudly donned their horse collars than did their steeds.

resources not only on behalf of guests, but also in a variety of other activities. The period between 1930 and 1960 saw increased concentration on streamlining the farms and the sale of products of the land, and more intensive efforts to maintain the expected services to guests with a smaller staff. More and more college students and seasonal employees became part of Mohonk's fabric of service.

These were very active years for Bert Smiley's wife, Mabel Craven Smiley. For a long period she lent her guidance in matters of housekeeping and employee relations. During her more than sixty years of continuous residence at Mohonk, the welfare of employees was one of her special concerns. She was interested in their recreational needs and helped arrange for parties and library facilities. She also served as an unofficial but much appreciated counselor for both personal and business problems until her death in 1972.

Over the years Mohonk employees engaged in diverse activities, including baseball teams, variety shows, and even a band. Supported by management, on-site recreational activities for employees gained backing, while the baseball team was supported by guests for whom it served as entertainment. Most employees had no means of transportation to go off the mountain (current employees are largely commuters), so group activities were a key part of residential life and well-being at Mohonk.

The Smileys' appreciation for employee morale has been demonstrated throughout their ownership of Mohonk. The balcony of the Mountain House Parlor

LAKE MOHONK BASEBALL TEAM—SEASON OF 1916

H. DELAMATER
Manager

Standing—G. Owl, Pitcher and Center Field; O. D. Neil, 2d Base;
R. Terwilliger, 1st Base; C. Juckett, Catcher; C. Turner, 3d Base.
Kneeling—H. Delamater, Center Field; J. Davis, Left Field;
P. Howland, Right Field; W. Churchill, Short Stop and Pitcher.

DAVID OWL
Captain
and Pitcher

Mohonk's baseball team played on the mountain against fiercely competitive local teams. Work schedules did not permit employees to engage in off-site competition.

The Mohonk Band, pictured here in 1921, gathered musical talents from many departments; it included a gardener, a driver, and several carpenters.

was originally installed so that employees might enjoy the rich and varied musical, cultural, and educational programs of the house.

In 1907, Picnic Lodge was conceived by Hugh Smiley and built with the express goal of having a place for employees to congregate socially, as well as partake in refreshments and buy sundries. In a 1920 *Bulletin*, Picnic Lodge is described as the location of the "Mohonk Stores," highlighting its "General Store" role for House guests, day visitors, and employees, where soda, food, and personal items could be purchased. In 1978, after a period of inactivity, Picnic Lodge once again was renovated for employee use, as well as being a center for day visitors.

PICNIC LODGE, MOHONK LAKE, N. Y.

Picnic Lodge, c. 1915.

As the 1930s drew to a close, the third generation of Smileys reached adulthood. Dan, Keith, and Gerow Smiley were forming their future lives. They met their future wives at Mohonk and married within several years of each other—Keith Smiley to Ruth Happel in 1939, Dan Smiley to Alice Plumlee in 1939, and Gerow Smiley to Marion Bonnell in 1943. Six of their children were born between 1941 and 1945, and the last two by 1953. Those eight children would spend some or all of their childhood living on the mountain.

Marion Bonnell Smiley

Marion Bonnell was hired by Mohonk in 1939 as part of a large wait staff serving guests. She married Gerow Smiley soon after, in 1943. After starting her family, Marion continued to dedicate herself to the enterprise. She worked in a broad range of jobs, off and on, over the next seventy years—kitchen steward's office, front office, administrative housekeeper, gift shop, archives volunteer—"wherever there was a need."

As Marion described her wait staff duties:

Waitresses were trained by working their way up the hierarchy of the dining rooms—starting in the girls' dining room. The next step up was the officers' room, then the children's and finally the Main Dining room.

Waitresses had to wear uniforms with long sleeves; white during the day and black at night. They also wore stockings, aprons and hair nets. They had to wash their own uniforms. There was an overall emphasis in the dining room on quiet, dignified dining. Guests "dressed up" for meals. If a waitress dropped a tray, shattering the quiet, she had to wash a window! Guests were assigned to a particular table and kept it throughout their stay, regardless of what time they came to meals. They also had the same waitress throughout, although if they were not pleased with their spot they asked to change and every effort would be made to accommodate them.

Marion Bonnell was raised on a farm in nearby Grahamsville, where she attended a one-room schoolhouse through eighth grade. Upon graduation from high school in Liberty, New York, she came directly to Mohonk, where three of her eight siblings were already working.

Above: Marion Bonnell among her coworkers. Marion is in the back row of the bottom group photograph (number 12, although the 12 was actually written on the right shoulder of the woman in front of her). See enlargement of Marion's image at left. Little did she know when she arrived for a summer job in 1939 that she would marry a Smiley and be involved with Mohonk for the rest of her life.

Ruth Happel Smiley

Ruth Happel first came to Mohonk in 1936 as a guest with her parents. At age twenty-two she had earned a master's degree in horticulture and landscape design from Cornell University. Ruth found a perfect match for her talents and her passion for botany when she married Keith. With her horticultural expertise she was well qualified to oversee the Mohonk gardens. Over the following decades she gently guided the succession of head gardeners and kept them aligned with Mohonk's reverence for the natural environment. Ruth's regularly scheduled garden walks and nature walks were very popular with guests, as were her evening slide presentations. She remained active at Mohonk for over fifty years as resident horticul-

turist, naturalist, nature photographer, and author of two books and numerous booklets and articles.

Ruth employed her photography skills and artist's eye as a means to engage guests more directly with the natural world around them. In her own words: "Nature's moods and patterns are constantly changing. You can take pictures of 'things,' but it doesn't necessarily create a mood or reaction. The critical moment is when the viewer's sensitivity is touched by the artist's eye—and a kind of magic occurs. ….. What's been most important to me over the years is knowing that I've helped open people's eyes, helped them see and appreciate nature. In an age when we are becoming more removed from this good earth, such appreciation is a touchstone, a sense of stewardship that unites us all."

Recently, some of Ruth's "art of nature" series of photographs have become framed artworks, gracing the walls of guest rooms and throughout the spa.

Photo: Rudy Simmon

Left: Ruth Smiley in the Mohonk Garden.

Right: Ruth Smiley was an avid photographer.

Alice Plumlee Smiley

In the spring of 1938, Rachel Smiley brought Alice Plumlee, a professional violinist from Juilliard School of Music, to perform in concerts through the fall season.

It didn't take long for Dan Smiley to "discover" Alice, and they married the following year. She continued her music performances in the seasonal parlor concerts, and during the remaining months contributed in a variety of other activities. As Alice later described:

> I observed early on that Smiley women learned how to answer a variety of needs in this remarkable place, and to do what came to hand. Among other things, I remember teaching piano to both schoolboys and employees; making Christmas decorations for the winter dining room; trying without spectacular success to run a nightly entertainment program for our few winter guests; and, in the 1950s, decorating three sample guestrooms on a very limited budget, as possible models to copy in quantity.

Alice also remembered vividly the challenges of World War II, both in aiding in wartime efforts and helping the business survive. During the war years, family members and employees spent evening sessions sewing infant and hospital supplies to send to the American Friends Service Committee. During these rough years there were national shortages of workers and supplies, and Mohonk was as directly affected by food rationing as individual citizens. The food shortages caused staff and family members to help in food production for the Mountain House, by any means possible.

Portrait of Alice Plumlee Smiley painted by her cousin Rachel Smiley Matteson, c. 1950.

Photo: Keldon Polacco

Ruth, Marion, and Alice Smiley each became valued leaders and organizers of Mohonk theme programs. Ruth was involved in Garden Holiday, Hikers Holiday, and Photographer's Holiday for many decades; Marion led the Pioneer Weekend in the mid-1970s; and Alice created and ran the popular and profitable October Fest of Chamber Music from 1976 to 1992. ∾

Right: Alice Smiley assisting with maple syrup production in 1942; 400 maple trees had been tapped, and special copper pans were built in order to boil the sap outdoors.

Below: Alice Smiley's war ration book.

Photo: Daniel Smiley, Jr.

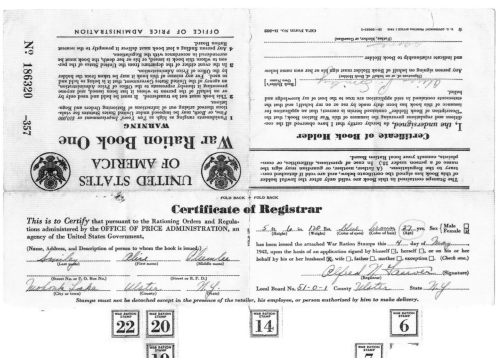

≈ 13 ≈

A New Business Order

"Her serenity of outlook undergirded the efforts of other members of the family, as they struggled successively with … Depression, world war, rationing, and inflation."

A. Keith Smiley, describing Effie Smiley, 1953

With the death of Daniel's wife, Effie Smiley, on May 14, 1951, a chapter in Mohonk's history closed. Guests, employees, and family members who knew her came away impressed with her kindly spirit, gentle manner, and strong supportive qualities. From 1880 to 1950, Effie helped shape the growth of Mohonk as a resort and the expansion of its influence. She knew presidents and foreign ministers, famous artists, and imposing merchants. Yet her modest and winning ways treated all alike, whether employee, guest, or conference delegate. During the Depression years and World War II, when all America saw old ways and many traditions knocked into a "cocked hat," Effie Smiley provided a personal continuity while her family sought to change, to modify, and to face mounting expenses while maintaining the quality and the core of Mohonk's purposes and guest services. Effie experienced the coming of electric lights and automobiles, massive social upheavals, and the birth of the nuclear age. She also saw that Mohonk—its outlook in seeking harmony between people and between people and nature—still remained "Mohonk."

In anticipation of the day when leadership would change in the business, Bert and Francis began to plan for succession. In 1953, Bert and Francis's partnership expanded to include Bert's sons, Daniel and Keith, and Francis's son, Gerow. The expanded proprietorship was part of a shift from personal ownership to a more modern business structure.

Bert and Francis saw to the operations and the comfort of guests. Bert also advised on finance and the park department. Francis concentrated on accounting, engineering, and grounds. Dan served as controller and saw to engineering, as well as to purchasing building and grounds materials. Keith gave attention to the "front of the house," advertising, and *The Mohonk Bulletin*, while Gerow applied his energies to personnel and farm operations.

While carrying out their increased responsibilities, the three younger partners were also raising their families on the mountain.

The partners and a number of key staff members lived in Cottage Grove and other housing near the Mountain House. Their children played together, and the families formed a close community.

Francis and Rachel Smiley family members, 1949—Franny, Marion, Gerow, Patricia, Rachel, Doc, Francis.

Photo: Albert K. Smiley, II

Photo: Albert K. Smiley, II

Bert and Mabel Smiley grandchildren,
1949—Sandra, Dan, Anna, Pril, Bert.

Breakfast cookout, c. 1950,
served by resident manager
Judson W. Bunnell and
family members Gerow,
Dan, and Doc Smiley.

Sharing mountain life together, young Smileys gravitated toward interesting work sites and workers, and idolized certain staff members. Outdoor Supervisor Alton Quick, known as Quickie, was a particular favorite. Fourth-generation Bert Smiley has fond memories of participating in Quickie's outdoor chores, whether riding in the snowplow or operating the bulldozer controls. When Bert was a little older, Quickie taught him to use firearms to hunt woodchucks (woodchuck holes in fields being dangerous for horses).

Alyce Whalen Bailey, daughter of Frank Whalen, head of the Power House, also has fond memories of Quickie. She grew up on the mountain in a house near his, and remembers the

From 1948 to his death in 1964, second-generation Bert Smiley created annual department photographs of Mohonk employees. His seven-year-old grandson, also named Bert Smiley, is in the center of this 1951 photograph to the left of Alton Quick, Outdoor Supervisor.

great fun of sledding all the way down the mountain for two miles on Mossy Brook Road and sometimes being lucky enough to encounter Quickie at the bottom. He would "let us tie our sleds on the back of the coal trucks and hitch a ride back up the mountain." The sled ride down took about twenty minutes; the truck ride up took about ten minutes.

Generations of Smileys growing up at Mohonk have engaged in many aspects of the hotel operations and activities. Such experience has been of direct benefit to the business, as descendants have later become employees, managers, or board members.

Growing up as part of the Mohonk community, it is not unusual for Smiley family members to work in nearly every department of the organization. An excellent example is Sandra Smiley's list of her Mohonk jobs over the years: babysitter, flower girl, switchboard operator, swimming instructor, afternoon tea server, relish girl, relief waitress, rustic carpenter, Picnic Lodge supervisor, Shiatsu masseuse, housekeeping floor supervisor, Granary checker, coordinator of Holistic Way programs, information desk attendant, coordinator of summer ministers, archives assistant, library manager, and leader of early-morning meditation walks and boat rides.

Pril Smiley serves guests at the Granary's first year of operation in 1964.

Fourth-generation Sandra Smiley thatches a summerhouse roof with local reed grass, 1979.

The 1950s ushered in a host of improvements at Mohonk, including the first electric power supplied by the Central Hudson Gas & Electric Corporation rather than by the Mohonk power plant. Prior generations keenly desired to remain independent of public utilities, but by mid-century Mohonk's utilities were wearing out and failing to meet current needs. In 1958 the Mountain House was rewired to convert it from the older direct current power to the alternating current supplied by Central Hudson.

Other investments in infrastructure had to be made shortly thereafter. Renovation of the Grove Building section of the Mountain House followed the relocation of the Mohonk School to Cragsmoor in 1958. The hydraulic elevator was replaced with two electrically powered elevators in the late 1960s. These upgrades were essential, but were also a significant financial strain.

During this period the Smileys realized that changing times necessitated a new approach toward conferences. Some groups were not drawn to Mohonk as a meeting site because of the restrictive customs, but a great variety of other organizations used Mohonk's facilities and ambience for important meetings. Over 100 different YMCA conferences met at Mohonk over the years. Other groups included the Layman's Foreign Mission Inquiry, New York State Library Association, the Conference on Science, Philosophy and Religion, American Telephone and Telegraph Company executives, an institute on cancer research, an assortment of local and regional agencies, and a number of industry workshops and training sessions.

As the social upheavals of the 1960s approached, it was not an easy time for Mohonk, but thanks to a penchant for grappling with change it became a fruitful time, culminating with Mohonk's centennial that focused on Mohonk's second century.

Recognition

Francis G. Smiley died peacefully on July 14, 1962. His death was unexpected and filled the hearts of guests and employees alike with much sadness. In *The Mohonk Bulletin* a special memorial was printed:

Some people's lives are like a pebble dropped in the ocean. Such was the life of Francis Gerow Smiley. Lived in one small spot with quiet integrity, intense loyalty, a devotion to duty which defies description, and a thoroughly delightful sense of humor, it has yet affected untold thousands of guests, who, through the years, have carried home with them the blessings of his gentle presence. For some, the memories will center on his kindly advice with their fishing problems; for others, it will be the spiritual benefits of his conduct of the daily Morning Prayer service which will remain.

We are grateful for his years of service, and the warmth of his life, which will linger on with that of his father and uncle, to become an integral part of the "spirit of Mohonk."

In 1964 Mohonk friends, in gratitude for the life and work of Francis Smiley, contributed in his memory a new Allen organ for the Parlor. There the sounds of music serve as a reminder of the service and dedication that Francis gave to Mohonk and his role in assuring its survival.

Only two years later, Mohonk's friends would again be saddened, this time by the news of Albert "Bert" Smiley's death on November 9, 1964. For over fifty years Bert Smiley, like his brother Francis, wrestled with the dual challenge of keeping a family business running while seeking a balance between survival and the higher motives behind Mohonk's purpose. Excerpts from his correspondence reveal that he and his relatives sought always to follow Daniel's dictum that "guests should never see the wheels turning."

For those who might have the impression that owning Mohonk was, or is, all sweetness and joy, an enclave apart from life's grueling realities, they need only peruse Bert's correspondence files to correct such misimpressions. The following excerpt from a letter to his father strikes a responsive chord in those people today who feel overwhelmed by the mountain of paper and electronic mail:

There is much food for thought in this letter of thine, as in many others, but so far, I have not had much time to do the necessary thinking. Although I am making a real effort to carry out the arrangement of my work, according to thy suggestions,

I am afraid I am not making much progress, and at times I am considerably discouraged in my inability to delegate very much of the work to others. In these times, at least, I think it is best to interview the employees myself; and besides that I really enjoy getting around the country a little, especially with the car, and it gets me away from the grind at the desk and the everlasting memorandums and reports that have grown so now that it is about one man's job to read them over and get them placed where they belong, let alone putting much time studying on them. If I had time to properly digest all the stuff it would be mighty pleasant and a great benefit to read them; but as it is, it seems to me just so much stuff every day to plow through and get rid of during the evening and between times.

Yet, through it all, the delights of having one's family amid such surroundings, the companionship of good friends, and the beauties of nature on the Mohonk property enlivened and gave purpose to both Francis's and Bert Smiley's lives.

In 1969 some of Mohonk's guests who through the years were close to Bert felt there should be some permanent memorial as a reminder of his love for and contributions to Mohonk. Remembering his interest in the outdoors, a committee led by long-time Mohonker Warren L. Cruikshank agreed with the Smiley family that a rose garden would be a suitable memorial. The Albert K. Smiley memorial rose garden, with a seat built of cedar from trees grown on Mohonk land, was dedicated on July 8, 1969, during Mohonk's 100th anniversary celebration. ❧

14
The Journey in Leadership
1910 – 1970

"It is doubtful that we could borrow the money, even if we had dared to do so."

A. Keith Smiley, on financial challenges of the 1960s

Decades after the deaths of the second-generation Smiley brothers, Francis and Bert, third-generation proprietors Dan and Keith reflected on the management eras that had passed before they took the helm. Their examination of the past became a most significant contribution to Mohonk's future survival. They wrote a number of memos to key advisors and to the board of directors summarizing the challenging years between 1910 and 1970. These memos outlined the lessons learned and the perspective gained in striving to find the balance between sticking to principles on one hand and effecting needed change on the other. Dan and Keith summarized their findings by decade.

In the decade of **1910–1920**, in spite of the World War, there was high occupancy in the five-month season (Mohonk was closed from November to May), and general maintenance was kept up quite well; Grandfather Daniel had assembled a team of young managers, some of whom were old enough by that time to be free of the draft. An innovative house manager named H.C. Phillips—a leader in the industry—developed personalized form letters and other methods of aggressive marketing.

1920–1930: Grandfather Daniel was still the head man in the twenties. The team of enterprising young managers whom Daniel had gathered and nurtured in the early 1900s had fragmented because of the war. H.C. Phillips had left to start his own business in 1922. His successor was allowed to cater to long-time guests with special rate deals, rather than implement marketing to encourage new business. The result: occupancy and volume of new business began to decline, and Mohonk began *its* depression at least five years prior to the beginning of the country's Great Depression. Hence, when it could have been a time of making profit and renovating, very little capital improvement took place. Daniel's grand development plan for a new dormitory and laundry complex never got beyond the drawing board. Sky Top Tower, completed in 1922, was the last major new building construction until the Conference House was built seven decades later.

1930–1940: The Great Depression notably took its toll on the business operation. New government restrictions and new insurance requirements necessitated certain changes. A program for installing automatic sprinklers had to be initiated. Soon after the Depression "struck," some staff were glad to work solely for room and board rather than be laid off for the winter. Guest occupancy was low, even in summer. Mohonk had to buy cheap furnishings that did not last well.

1940–1950: The World War II years challenged Mohonk in numerous ways. Very little in the way of furnishings or equipment was available outside the black market. Food shortages limited what the kitchen was able to offer guests. There were staff shortages in many departments, and maintenance and repair needs were seriously set back.

1950–1960: By this decade Dan, Keith, and Gerow had become partners. Dan was watching the accounting closely and also was in charge of the engineering crews. He was constantly warning that Mohonk needed to make more profit in order to concentrate on long-neglected upkeep. Additionally, guest needs were changing—more private bathrooms were required—

I think to most of your real, ardent Mohonk guests, these accommodations would be welcome because we would feel Mohonk's future would be better insured."

Since the day-to-day management of the business had been reduced to two Smiley partners of the third generation, reorganization became a necessity. Dan and Keith Smiley sought wise counsel from selected friends, associates, and professionals connected with, and dedicated to, Mohonk's philosophy and mission. Out of extensive legal, family, and personal discussions came a new business structure—Smiley Brothers, Inc., organized in 1969. Forming the board of directors marked the first time that the Smiley partners positioned within the corporate structure outside professionals with business experience to help steer Mohonk forward. Thus a broadened base of leadership was created with an entity that was directly responsible for Mohonk's ongoing sustainability.

The charter board of directors included family members Daniel Smiley, Keith Smiley, and Gerow Smiley, and each of their oldest sons of the fourth generation—Dan C. Smiley, Bert Smiley, and Doc Smiley. It also included Benjamin Matteson (married to Rachel Smiley Matteson), and four non-family businessmen.

The first action of the Board of Directors of Smiley Brothers, Inc. was to elect Benjamin H. Matteson as executive vice president of the new corporation, with the responsibilities of general manager. Ben had grown up in New Paltz, where his father taught at the state university, so he was familiar with the long-held connections between the town and university and the Smiley family. Ben's marriage to Rachel gave him an appreciation of Mohonk's philosophy and an understanding of its organizational challenges. Before coming to Mohonk he was employed at the nearby branch of IBM as a mechanical engineer associated with computer development and technical management. His business acumen, strategic planning skills, and friendly mien with guests provided exactly what Mohonk needed to shift the momentum and strengthen the business.

Benjamin H. Matteson served as Mohonk's lead executive from 1969 to 1985. Bert Smiley later commented, "Ben really gave us the spark that allowed us to carry on and prosper during those years … He gave us the confidence we could change with the times."

It did not take Ben long to delve headlong into his new responsibilities. In the first board of directors meeting in March 1969—three months after being hired—Ben summarized his activities. The minutes state:

> Mr. Matteson reported that after starting work for Smiley Brothers in January, he had consulted experts on resorts and in business management. Their unqualified opinion, after visiting Mohonk, was that the resort had great potential for financial success and guest satisfaction as a "unique landmark of antiquity." This judgment recognized the limiting factors of some of Mohonk's traditions and the present condition of its physical plant. These things could be capitalized. Certain needs were recognized: an aggressive advertising and selling campaign conducted in a manner appropriate to Mohonk's policies; rebuilding a regular summer guest clientele (not groups), supplemented by groups <u>and</u> regular guests at other times of year; a team of managers as the organization framework; and an accounting system tailored to the changing management need of <u>this</u> resort.

Ben Matteson's strong leadership and thoughtful game plan enabled Mohonk to enter the 1970s with a renewed sense of purpose and optimism. ❧

~ 15 ~
Toward the Second Century

"Our 100th year is the springboard to our second century."

The Mohonk Bulletin, June 1, 1969

As Mohonk prepared to celebrate its 100th anniversary, the time was propitious for reflecting upon the wisdom of the past while implementing plans for the future. The stewardship of earlier generations had been augmented in varied forms of service by later family members. First-generation Albert and Daniel Smiley had arrived at a simple formula for operating Mohonk—integrity in all dealings, moderation in all things, protection of the land, resistance to fads of the moment in favor of timeless virtues, and catering to the whole person rather than just to the need for entertainment. It was a formula modern, even daring, in its time. As seen through the pages of this story, it was an ethic severely tested by the whims of society and the realities of wartime and Depression, spiraling inflation, and energy crises. Though this formula set Mohonk apart, it became the irresistible draw that beckoned people to come back again and again.

As the June 1, 1969, *Mohonk Bulletin* proclaimed:

In years to come there will be more leisure than ever, and more money. Vacationists are going to demand much more than bars and bingo and double rooms with double baths. They will want challenge for the mind and growth for the spirit; they will demand good food and good company, but they will want it in an atmosphere which encourages the use of every sense we possess for the greater good of all; in sum, they will want re-creation rather than merely recreation.

Commemoration of Mohonk's Centennial in 1969 took a variety of forms and included numerous activities. Sunday, June 1, was a festival day. In the late afternoon the Smiley family and guests buried the Mohonk Centennial Time Capsule at the putting green. This sealed receptacle contains a variety of Mohonk artifacts of the 1969 era. In accordance with the notice on the plaque, which was subsequently placed on the rock beside the site, it is to be opened at the end of the next one hundred years, in 2069. The Reverend Ralph E. Davis then commented upon Mohonk, its meaning and its future. Following the time capsule exercises, the Smileys invited all guests and visitors to a reception and refreshments in the Lake Lounge. A buffet supper was provided in the Main Dining Room amidst colorful decorations befitting the occasion.

Rachel O. Smiley and Southwick Vietor celebrating Mohonk's 100th anniversary.

Following after-dinner coffee in the Lake Lounge and a song service, a panel of Smiley family members and friends discussed the highlights of the first century and peered into the possible developments of the second.

On the evening of June 6 there occurred a ceremony in recognition of the 75th anniversary of the first of the series of Conferences on International Arbitration, which took place annually from 1895 through 1916. Featured talks included: reminiscences by retired journalist Louis P. Lochner, who had attended the 1914 conference; Noel J. Brown, Political Affairs Officer with the United Nations, who delivered remarks on the "Present World Situation"; and comments by Warren F. Kuehl, professor of history at the University of Akron in Ohio, regarding the significance of the conferences.

Other highlights of the 100th anniversary included the dedication of the Albert K. (Bert) Smiley Memorial Rose Garden, and an address in the Parlor by the Reverend Ralph W. Sockman with appropriate reminiscences about his years at Mohonk and relationships with the Smiley family. There was also a host of special programs, both entertaining and of a serious nature, during the course of the summer.

Keith and Dan Smiley burying the Centennial Time Capsule on the putting green, 1969.

These were announced in a special newspaper, *The Mohonk Chronicle*, formatted in the spirit of a New Paltz village news sheet of a hundred years earlier.

With the 100th anniversary year completed, a definite sense of renewed interest and kinetic energy could be felt at Mohonk. The transition from the 1960s to the 1970s proved to be a time of great significance and challenges in the unfolding story of Mohonk. ❧

Mohonk's centennial was celebrated throughout its four seasons, with winter events and offerings featured in a special brochure.

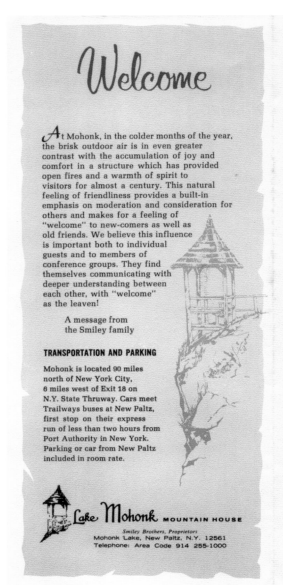

16

Stewards of the Land

"This process is in keeping with the long-standing intent of the Smiley family and Mohonk Mountain House to preserve the natural beauty and historic features of our outlying lands … and to protect these lands from future development."

Bert Smiley, on the philosophy of land transfers, 2011

When founder Albert Smiley first considered purchasing the Mohonk property, it was the landscape around Mohonk Lake that captivated him—not John Stokes's tavern. It was impossible not to be in awe of so many spectacular natural features concentrated in one place—a mountain lake, dramatic rock formations, primeval forest, and views of mountains and valleys in every direction.

After the initial 280-acre land purchase, the Smiley brothers realized that, going forward, they needed to extend their land holdings as much as possible to prevent the encroachment of development. They first acquired parcels in the Trapps and Bonticou areas, and in the early 1900s concentrated on adding farmlands to the resort holdings. As many of the nearby farms became abandoned because of the lure of city life or the richer farmlands of the Midwest, the Smiley family eventually pieced together a mosaic of over 100 farms. Over time many of the open fields reverted to forest land, because some of the farms had been long-abandoned.

Through the first half of the 1900s, the Smileys continued to purchase land to further protect the overall estate and to enable expanded construction of the vast road and trail network that was a direct benefit to the Mohonk guests and visitors. By mid-century the property encompassed 7,500 acres. However, the business began having difficulty supporting such a large estate. The Mountain House did not produce sufficient income to take care of the entire tract, and yet the Smiley family remained united in its opposition to the idea of the land becoming fodder for developers. The answer, after much discussion with trusted friends, financial advisors, and attorneys, lay in forming a private not-for-profit corporation called The Mohonk Trust—later called the Mohonk Preserve.

Brothers Dan and Keith Smiley spearheaded this endeavor. In 1963 the preserve was established. There was excitement in formulating its objectives and testing new concepts of land stewardship that embraced education, scientific study, inspiration, and recreation. A stated mission was "the improvement and understanding of man's relationship to man, and man's relationship to nature," thus formally enshrining the original philosophy of founder Albert K. Smiley. From the early days of the preserve's founding, Dan's activity gravitated to its scientific and education work, and his brother Keith's to Mohonk's human networking tradition and world peace.

An immediate objective of the preserve was to acquire and serve as steward of certain very special Mohonk lands not essential to the operation of the

Keith Smiley, 1963.

Dan Smiley, 1975.

Photo: Pril Smiley

resort. Dan Smiley likened this to "the American Indian concept of communal ownership of the mountain land" and declared that a "serendipitous result was that it became the turning point in the history of Shawangunk land ownership." He surmised that "for the first time since the days of the American Indians, *women* took (not were given) an active part in matters to do with the land." The founding gift that established the preserve was made by Dan's and Keith's mother, Mabel C. Smiley. Dan's wife, Virginia Viney Smiley, asked to be a founding trustee, and other women—Ruth H. Smiley (Mrs. Keith), Rachel O. Smiley (Mrs. Francis), and Rachel Smiley Matteson followed as members of the board.

Selected tracts of the outlying resort lands were gradually sold to the preserve, beginning with a 487-acre Trapps parcel in 1966. This represented to outsiders an astounding decision by the family—selling land at a price significantly less than what Albert Smiley paid in purchasing the original acreage decades before. Ultimately the 5,300 acres sold to the preserve enabled the formation of a span of untouched wilderness along the Shawangunk Ridge from Gardiner to Rosendale. As Dan Smiley summarized, "The mere acquisition of land at Mohonk has never been an end in itself. From the earliest days there has been a blending of concern for preserving the beauty of the landscape and the integrity of the flora and fauna—with appropriate human use and enjoyment. There has been a feel for the land as a living organism, the sustainer of all life."

In 2011, Smiley Brothers, Inc. decided to divest itself of a tract of outlying land on the east side of the ridge. The 857 acres consisted of the historic Brook, Pine, and Kleinekill farms, along with the Testimonial Gateway. As with land transferred in the 1960s, this acreage was no longer integrated with Mountain House operations; current management energies needed to be concentrated on the core operation. The board of directors strongly favored a plan to assure that this iconic foothills farmland remain free from development. Fortuitously, the Open Space Institute (OSI) stepped in to acquire the property.

Established in 1974 to protect "scenic, natural, and historic landscapes," OSI partnered in protecting 2.2 million acres from New York to Maine. In the local region specifically, OSI invested heavily in a conservation initiative along the 50-mile Shawangunk Ridge, protecting nearly 33,000 acres on the ridge through its first four decades.

Thus, a perfect partner came into Mohonk's land-use vision. The concept was for OSI to act as an intermediary and purchase the Smiley Brothers acreage with the stated intent

Part of the Trapps parcel sold to the Mohonk Preserve. Painting by Carl Werntz.

of continuing the traditional farming operations, protecting the property, and ultimately transferring the land to the Mohonk Preserve.

The Smiley family and the board of directors immediately recognized that an opportunity such as this was unlikely to come along again. The most important considerations were not only practical and financial, but philosophical, based on the Smiley's long-held land stewardship ethic. The board felt that the land must be protected, and that having the preserve ultimately become the stewards of this acreage would be a fortuitous outcome of the proposed transfer. During board discussions Bert Smiley observed that, while the family is unapologetically emotional in their attachment to the Mohonk lands, there is unanimous agreement that ultimately stewardship is much more important than private ownership.

Gerow Smiley, as one of the last third-generation family members remaining, offered his perspective on the significance of the land being transferred. He recalled that when the Testimonial Gateway was constructed in 1907, it marked the entrance to the Mohonk property. At that time guests travelled to Mohonk via this early approach route, passing through the archway of this structure. The view through the arch perfectly framed the span of the ridge ahead, over which carriages transported guests to the Mountain House. It was the "gateway to Mohonk." Gerow emphasized that he supported the land transfer because the view through the archway would now have an even more poignant and far-reaching meaning, as it would provide a "gateway to the Smileys' vision of the land."

Sky Top Mohonk. Painting by Bayard Henry Tyler.

As part of this land transfer process, the crucial third partner, the Mohonk Preserve, pledged to raise funds to purchase the OSI acquisition on a fair, well-thought-out basis over three or more years. As hoped for, in 2014 the preserve entered into a purchase agreement with OSI for the entire acreage. The transfer is now complete, and the preserve manages these lands as the "Mohonk Foothills." There was notable satisfaction in being able to continue the vision of the preserve's founders.

Today the Mohonk Preserve encompasses over 8,000 acres of cliffs, forests, and farmland. It is an important feature in the Mid-Hudson Valley region, attracting over 200,000 visitors annually, including hikers, naturalists, rock climbers, cross-country skiers, bicyclists, school groups, photographers, and many other nature enthusiasts, including guests staying at the Mountain House.

Open Space Institute award

On October 31, 2011, members of the Smiley family gathered at the Metropolitan Club in New York City to receive the 2011 Open Space Institute Land Conservation Award presented to the Smiley family and Mohonk Mountain House. Kim Elliman, CEO of OSI, stated:

On behalf of our Chairman John Adams and the OSI Board, welcome to our annual luncheon when we honor an outstanding conservationist. ... This year we gather to honor the Smiley family of Mohonk. Landowners in the Hudson River Valley for almost 150 years, the Smileys pioneered conservation in New York State, and therefore in the nation, and they also established among the country's first desti-nation hotels—at Mohonk and Minnewaska. In so doing, they have protected the heart of the Shawangunks, which lies at the center of the Hudson Valley. ... Of the 130,000 acres OSI has protected in New York State, one quarter lies in the Shawan-gunks, and Mohonk dominates the landscape, just as the Smileys have dominated conservation there. ... Thirty years ago, a bold OSI board embarked on a program to preserve the Gunks. What we know now, which we didn't 150 years ago or even 30 years ago, is that the Shawangunk Ridge promises to be a critical connection for wildlife, particularly as our climate changes. ... It is a key link running down to the Kittatinnys in New Jersey, the Blue Mountains in Pennsylvania, the Shenandoah and Blue Ridge Mountains of Virginia and ultimately to the Southern Appalachians. …We are honored to have worked with the Smileys to conserve so much of this iconic landscape. Just two weeks ago, OSI acquired another 1,000 acres at the foot of Mohonk, farmland, most of it from the Smileys, to ensure the viewshed and farms of the Wallkill Valley.

Bert Smiley accepted the award, with the following remarks:

On behalf of my family and the entire staff of Mohonk Mountain House, I want to say that we're honored by the recognition you've given us for our stewardship of the Shawangunk Ridge. Landscape conservation was a priority for [our founder] Albert

Wendy Smiley, Doc Smiley, Gerow Smiley, Terri Smiley, Shanan Smiley, Robyn Gullickson, Nina Smiley, Eric Gullickson, Tom Smiley, Pril Smiley, Bert Smiley, & Keith LaBudde.

from day one, which ultimately led to the acquisition of seventy-five hundred acres of mountaintop land in the original Mohonk estate.

At Mohonk Mountain House our mission is to provide opportunities for re-creation and renewal of body, mind, and spirit in a beautiful natural setting. Indeed, the entire layout of Mohonk from its earliest days, with the Mountain House at the center, and the trail and carriage road network radiating out from there, was designed to draw people out into the more remote parts of the property.

Back in the late 1800s when Mohonk was founded, the dominant method of land protection was acquisition by private individuals, as in the case of Albert and Alfred. As time passed and the need for other vehicles of conservation emerged, my family founded the Mohonk Preserve ... and ultimately transferred more than 5,000 acres of the original Mohonk estate to the Preserve, which is now responsible for the stewardship of those lands.

I'm happy to say that, in our latest chapter of landscape conservation, Mohonk Mountain House has conveyed 857 acres to OSI to ensure the protection in perpetuity of these lands, and to provide further opportunities for passive recreation and enjoyment, education, scientific research, and sustainable farming, in partnership with the Mohonk Preserve. My family and I are extremely honored and grateful that OSI has chosen to partner with the Mountain House and the Preserve to make possible the achievement of our long-term goals for this magnificent landscape. ❧

❧ 17 ❧

Renaissance — the 1970s

"I think our guests come to Mohonk seeking closeness to nature and tranquility of spirit."

Rachel O. Smiley, 1979

A remarkable resurgence of interest in history and an appreciation for the style and culture out of our past became a strong trend in the 1970s. For once it seemed there was no conflict between old and new. The rediscovery by many Americans of the tessellated pattern of our heritage came alongside evolving lifestyles and customs. In such an atmosphere Mohonk was "rediscovered" by many people who marveled at it as something unique in American life. Designated in 1973 as a place of architectural and historical significance, the Mountain House is listed on the National Register of Historic Places by the United States Department of the Interior. A decade later the Mountain House and its structures became listed as a National Historic Landmark.

"In a sense, Mohonk has no rules, although the general public insists that we do," Daniel Smiley once observed. The "rules," he declared, were like English common law, made up by precedent according to the instinctive ideas and behavior of the guests themselves. From the beginning the guests brought a certain air of preferred habits and customs dictated by the attitudes of the time. The simplicity and open-mindedness of

Mohonk's tradition did not insist on a sharp, blind adherence to custom. Private automobiles, once banned, became ubiquitous. The no-arrivals-or departures-on-Sunday policy also became a relic of the past, and bridge and dancing were, for a time, staples in evening entertainment. The significant point is that the essential Mohonk of substance is adhered to by guests because the Smileys refused to become tied to procedures. It may be considered something short of a societal miracle that the following customs survived for several more decades: jackets (with ties preferred); the daily ten-minute worship service and the Sunday morning nondenominational religious service, and the Sunday evening hymn sing. The absence of a cocktail lounge was the one tradition that the Smiley family held onto the longest. In 1970 the board of directors applied for a liquor license, thereby taking the first step toward loosening the beverage policy restrictions. At first Mohonk only offered wine in the dining room during dinner. Guests continued to imbibe pre-dinner cocktails in their own rooms, from their own supplies, as had always been the practice. A favorite story from the years during which Mohonk was officially "dry" was when Francis Smiley—asked by a guest where a drink could be found at Mohonk—dryly replied, "knock on any guest door after 5 o'clock."

In earlier times, when guests made longer stays at the Mountain House, they were able to learn more on their own about the resources that could be enjoyed than those in later years who could only make brief visits. Even in the "less organized" years, members of the Smiley family and staff provided many opportunities to enjoy group activity, both indoors and out. There were regattas on the lake, bowling, golf, and tennis tournaments, nature walks, cave exploration, treasure hunts, and a variety of games and contests.

As summer visits shortened and more new people came to the mountain in all seasons, it became clear that many guests enjoyed being a part of groups that pursued additional interests and hobbies other than sports and games. Members of the Smiley family and their friends responded to this need, creating new kinds of programs that were especially compatible with their own individual avocations. Additionally, Mohonk staff offered holidays and weekends focusing on special topics. Before 1970 only eight of these "theme programs" existed, including long-standing programs such as Garden Holiday and Hikers Holiday. Under Ben Matteson's forward-thinking leadership, many new programs were created, greatly enhancing Mohonk's offerings: What's in the Winter Woods?; China Week;

Mohonk's Official Logo

Mohonk guests will recognize Mohonk's logo as the silhouette of a rustic gazebo, called a "summerhouse." Summerhouses became popular in the Victorian era—influenced especially by landscape designer Andrew Jackson Downing. These structures have dotted the Mohonk landscape since Alfred Smiley built the first one in 1870. At one time Mohonk maintained 155 summerhouses.

Under Ben Matteson's leadership, Mohonk's advertising consultants, Needham & Grohman, started using the summerhouse design as a distinct marketing logo. It first appeared in Mohonk's 1970 promotional materials, but in a broader sense this image had been used since the earliest Mohonk Mountain House years to identify and promote the facilities and services provided. For visitors, the summerhouses are both a destination and a ubiquitous presence. They are seen and enjoyed whether swimming in the lake, relaxing on a porch, strolling through the gardens, or hiking on the many trails and carriage roads.

THEN & NOW

EVERYTHING OLD IS NEW AGAIN | WHITTIER SUMMERHOUSE

Our summerhouses are just one of the things that make Mohonk truly unique. And in 2016, we brought one back. Whittier Outlook, just below Sky Top Tower, was built around 1898, but was difficult to maintain because of its cliffside location, and was subsequently removed. Our Rustic Crew rebuilt Whittier Outlook in 2016, giving it a new life on our mountaintop.

Whittier Outlook, circa 1916

Whittier Outlook, 2016

Mohonk's rustic carpentry crew researches, replicates, and rebuilds original iconic summerhouse designs on their original sites, as shown on this page from a marketing publication.

In 1983 Ben Matteson decided to trademark the summerhouse logo, and Mohonk applied to the Secretary of State of the State of New York to register the design as an official "Service Mark." The certificate lists the "Date First Used in New York State" and the "Date First Used Elsewhere in the U.S." as 1870—recognizing its use as a Mohonk symbol from the first year the Mountain House opened for business.

State of New York - Department of State

Certificate of Registration of Service Mark

I, GAIL S. SHAFFER, SECRETARY OF STATE OF THE STATE OF NEW YORK, do hereby CERTIFY that in accordance with the application filed in this office on the 1st day of August , 19 83 , the SERVICE MARK described below has been duly registered in this Department pursuant to Article 24 of the General Business Law, in behalf of Smiley Brothers, Inc. (NY corp)
Name
New Paltz, New York 12461
Address

Description of Service Mark and Services for which mark is used:

Design of a summerhouse

Used in connection with: Hotel, Restaurant, Recreation, Program and Conference Center Services.

Class No. 100	Registration No.	S-7560
Date of Registration: 8/24/83	Registration Expires:	8/24/93
Date First Used In NEW YORK STATE: 1870		
Date First Used Elsewhere In The U.S.: 1870		

Mohonk trademarked the summerhouse logo in 1983.

Photo: Helmut G. Horn

Left: Dynamite storage shed, constructed c. 1900 and tucked under a cliff so that if an accidental explosion occurred the percussion would not damage the Mountain House.

Below: Fountain, constructed in 1902 at guests' request as a commemoration to the Garden Wing building that stood at that site from 1875 until 1902. The fountain features a centerpiece of crystal quartz clusters, surrounded by lily pads and goldfish.

14956   THE GARDENS, LAKE MOHONK HOUSE.   COPR DETROIT PHOTOGRAPHIC CO.

It was deeply gratifying when the landmark commission accepted this request and granted a one-of-a-kind status in bestowing its landmark designation to the entire "larger" Mohonk.

On December 9, 1986, Smiley family members, guests, employees, and friends gathered in the Mountain House Parlor. Mohonk historian Larry Burgess served as master of ceremonies, introducing representatives from the Department of the Interior and New York State. They officially presented to Dan, Keith, and Gerow Smiley a bronze plaque naming Mohonk as a National Historic Landmark.

Dan Smiley summarized, "The National Historic Landmark recognition has served a Janus-like function for Mohonk. We are looking backward at the development of the relationship of Mohonk's natural, structural, and human heritage. We are looking forward to its continuing interpretation and perpetuation." ❧

Gerow Smiley, Bernard Gavin, Keith Smiley, and Dan Smiley presented with National Historic Landmark plaque.

19

The Conference Legacy Continues

"Peace is the wholeness created by right relationships with oneself, other persons, other cultures, other life, Earth and the larger whole of which all are a part."

United Nations Earth Charter

A core value of the Smiley family has always been the examination and improvement of human relationships with other humans and with the world in which we live. Since the beginning, Mohonk has proved to be an ideal setting to engage in that work. Guests on holiday can reconnect with the world through nature and with others during recreational activities or a quiet and relaxed conversation in a summerhouse gazebo. And although it was once possible to convene large groups for this kind of exploration and activism under the auspices of the resort business, in the modern era that work has become the domain of Mohonk Consultations, a not-for-profit Mohonk sister organization that evolved from its original roots within the Mohonk Preserve.

An embodiment of the Mohonk spirit, with the purpose of advancing human relations, Mohonk Consultations continues because it has been able to effect change. Rather than adhere to one topic, such as environmentalism or social justice, Consultations functions as a catalyst that seeks out stakeholders and gathers them in an egalitarian forum amidst inspiring surroundings to build communities, encourage worthy action, and mobilize for positive change. In short, Mohonk Consultations gets people together so they can brainstorm with each other.

Mohonk's conference legacy began in 1883 with the first Conference of the Friends of the Indians, followed by the first Mohonk International Arbitration Conference in 1895. Both conferences significantly influenced public policy until 1916, when the gloom of World War I halted the efforts.

The conference legacy continued in a new context when the Mohonk Preserve was established in 1963. Part of the motivation in creating the preserve was to maintain the Smiley family's role of actively encouraging a better life for human beings and peaceable relations among them. It was hoped that this combination of goals might be accomplished within the context of the interdependence of all life on our planet—humans, animals, plants, the forces of nature.

Intense desire to reinforce long-standing social concerns and a motivation to demonstrate that a valuable acreage of open space could be maintained for purposes of public benefit lay behind the conferences. Through a combination of donations and fees collected from visitors, funding was achieved. Hence the preserve, by the terms of its agreement, committed itself to two interrelated objectives—the improvement of human understanding and cooperation on a world basis, and fostering the concept that humans are part of the total web of life on Earth.

The first program to be sponsored by the preserve stemmed from its International Affairs international student consultations. Groups of foreign students gathered at Mohonk to discuss and evaluate their experience in the United States. The overall goal was to assist them in the development of skills and perspectives for an effective transition from their studies in the United States to useful careers and satisfying lives in their home countries. The preserve also co-hosted International Peace Academy seminars and discussions for United Nations diplomats, continuing the Smiley family interest and commitment to seeking peaceful solutions to world problems.

In 1978 the Mohonk Preserve was reorganized. It shifted its focus and resources more toward

Attendees of the 1914 Mohonk Conference on International Arbitration gather on the west lawn for a photograph.

Left: Keith Smiley (far left, kneeling) with a group of international students, 1960.

Below left: Winslow Shaw, Mohonk Preserve charter board member, U Thant, then secretary-general of the United Nations, and Keith Smiley.

Below: Keith Smiley and his daughter, Sandra Smiley, 1994.

stewardship of the Shawangunk Ridge land and less toward the world's social concerns. Keith Smiley envisioned a separate organization that would address relationships between people as well as with our environment. Thus it was that in 1980 he created Mohonk Consultations, Inc. This new organization aimed at broadening efforts to maintain the quality of social and environmental life in the wider Hudson Valley region.

Since 1980, Consultations has reached out to business, government, and education leaders in the Hudson Valley and formed collaborations with local colleges on social and environmental projects. Helen Vukasin, who had been involved in the organization since its inception, joined the board in 1985 to help carry Consultations work forward. Also in 1985, Keith Smiley's daughter, Sandra Smiley, joined the board and continues to be active. Other family members, including Sandra's cousins Patty Matteson, Louisa Finn, and Sidney Craven, have served on the board.

Mohonk Consultations' ongoing practice has been to offer forums and conferences on vital local issues, from environmental stewardship and crime prevention, to controlling suburban sprawl and protecting fresh water. In 2016 it revived the long-standing Smiley

2016 Peace Conference group gathered on the west lawn of Mohonk Mountain House.

Photo: Jim Smith Photography

Flags of many nations were placed along the approach to Mohonk Mountain House to welcome participants to the 2016 Peace Conference.

family tradition of hosting meetings to discuss global issues. During the conference, entitled Realizing a Culture of Peace, participants engaged in lively discussions exploring "peace building" at home and abroad.

The mission statement for Mohonk Consultations reads, "Our purpose is to help to bring about a clearer understanding of the interrelationship of all life on earth, emphasizing the need for sustainable use of all the earth's resources, including the human community, and to support the development of practical means to do so." ∾

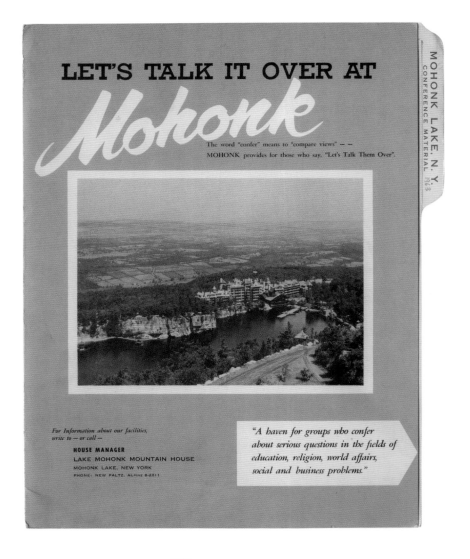

"Let's talk it over at Mohonk"—a phrase that echoes through Mohonk's entire history of welcoming conferences.

~ 20 ~

Values and Traditions Recast: A New Albert K. Takes Charge

"The cardinal aim of our business is the comfort and contentment of guests."

A.K. Smiley in a memorandum to staff, 1916

While noticeable strides had been made during the 1980s, the board continued to be concerned about the overall health of the business going forward, concerns that had by then become a perennial part of conducting business in a rapidly changing world. Low average guest occupancy and flagging group sales resulted in limited income. This was not helped by the continued restrictive alcoholic beverage policy, which created a sales and marketing handicap. The small profit that was realized overall was entirely plowed back into capital expenditures. The inherent high costs of maintaining the Mountain House and its many other structures—in addition to the extensive land holdings and road networks—drained any modest financial surplus that the resort operation generated.

In 1988, Smiley Brothers Board President Bert Smiley presented a comprehensive, long-range master plan for the future of Mohonk. His plan identified key areas of focus: a market study to assess potential new sources of guest business; an engineering study to determine the costs of improvements to the Mountain House; a business plan to bring together the market and engineering studies; a financial plan necessary to execute the above; and a stewardship plan for the Mohonk lands. Management was aware of Mohonk's increasingly diverse clientele that desired expanded food and beverage offerings, upscale amenities, and shopping opportunities. Foremost in the plan were efforts to increase guest occupancy, with a focus on improving meeting space, seeking group business, and attracting guests during the winter season.

The board of directors embraced Bert's plan and began to set goals and to form strategies for achieving higher standards in marketing, facilities, and guest service areas. To attract new guests, innovative theme weekends were added to the list of programs. Festival of the Arts—founded in 1989 by third-generation family member Patricia Smiley Guralnik and her pianist husband Robert Guralnik—quickly became a major annual summer event offering six weeks of music, theater, and dance presentations. A broader range of new guest activities was initiated to appeal to wider interests, including the "Mohonk Kid's Club," which was launched to expand children's activities. The completion of the Conference House in 1990, nestled among trees at the eastern end of the lake, represented a new focus on attracting conferences and business retreats. In keeping with Mohonk's tradition, the Conference House captured the spirit of earlier architectural styles by blending in with the natural surroundings.

Because of the recommendations, an important policy change finally came about when the long-held restrictions on alcoholic beverage service were gradually phased out. In 2005 Mohonk Mountain House opened the Carriage Lounge, its first cocktail lounge.

In the autumn of 1990, the period of non-family leadership drew to a close when Bert and his wife, Nina Feldman Smiley, volunteered to step in and dedicate themselves to continuing the tradition of Smiley family management of the business. Their careers and skills positioned them to be of immediate benefit to Mohonk. Bert came with a Ph.D. in economics from Princeton and job experience as an economist and director of research with the U.S. Department of Justice in Washington, D.C. Nina acquired her Ph.D. in social/developmental psychology from Princeton and had gained broad marketing research and public relations experience in the Washington D.C. area.

Bert and Nina Smiley. In her article "Moving to the Mountain—Sketches of my New Life at Mohonk," Nina, as director of marketing, noted that she found, "the content of my education is unfailingly useful in understanding the 'people side' and the 'product side' of this service industry."

Their move to Mohonk ushered in a new era. Bert assumed the role of CEO, while Nina became the new director of marketing. Leadership roles on the board of directors had already shifted to fourth-generation Smiley family members during this time, with Dan Smiley as chairman, Bert Smiley as president, and Pril Smiley as secretary and treasurer. Many others of their generation were also involved with Mohonk. The board continued to be strengthened through the 1990s with the addition of highly qualified, non-family directors, and several fifth-generation family members were elected to the board in 2000. During recent decades, sixth-generation Smileys have been growing up on the mountain—which is notable, since fewer than 3 percent of

family businesses in America succeed to the fourth generation of family involvement.

Mohonk's 125th anniversary in 1994 refocused attention on the sense of stewardship perpetuated by the Smiley family. There were renewed efforts to maintain the integrity of the physical structures, manage lands in an environmentally sensitive way, and emphasize the interaction of guests with each other and with nature. A great honor came to Mohonk Mountain House and the Smiley family during its quasquicentennial celebration when the United Nations Environment Programme recognized them with an award "for generations of dedicated leadership and commitment to the protection and enhancement of the environment and for their

Bert Smiley and Keith Smiley accepting the United Nations Environment Programme Award from Noel Brown (right), in 1994.

inestimable contribution to the cause of peace, justice, and sustainable human development."

During the last decade of the twentieth century, the newly energized management team found significant ways to enhance Mohonk's offerings, with an emphasis on providing new facilities for overnight guests during all four seasons. By way of example, more families were visiting Mohonk during the winter season, and the increasing variables of extreme weather necessitated more consistently reliable winter activities. In 1999 the board of directors authorized a major capital expenditure for a new facility intended primarily as a skating pavilion, with a refrigerated ice surface enabling skating from November through April. Conceived as a multipurpose venue for hosting year-round special events, the pavilion sits several hundred feet from the Mountain House and above the lake. The overall design and materials maintained the traditional Mohonk aesthetic.

Increased requests from guests for the relaxation and renewal provided by massage treatments led Mohonk's management to plan for a new facility that would honor Mohonk's holistic traditions while incorporating twenty-first-century services that reflected change in spa concepts from across the world. Six hundred tons of conglomerate rock were excavated from the site and "recycled" into the stone walls, fireplaces, and retaining walls of the Spa wing. The new wing opened in 2005, adding 30,000 square feet of new space at a cost of $14 million, dramatically changing the length and roofline of the Mountain House.

Or did it? The architecture was so effective—using stone and wood blended with the existing nineteenth-

Photo: Jim Smith Photography

The pavilion design incorporates architectural features of the Parlor Wing and uses generous amounts of Shawangunk conglomerate rock for its pillars and for the 39-foot-tall fireplace.

It took dynamite and heavy equipment—blasting down through twenty-five feet of bedrock—to create the lower spa level that houses the pool.

and early-twentieth-century buildings—that it seemed as if it had been part of Albert and Daniel Smiley's original vision. "The Spa was built to look 100 years old the day it opened," noted Nina Smiley, Mohonk's marketing director.

A geothermal system uses the constant temperature of the earth to heat and cool the building, and a green-roofed area is used for meditation and yoga. Inside, two, 80-foot-long enclosed verandas connect to a solarium with a stone fireplace and provide breathtaking views. The pool, with its expansive windows and views of the spectacular surroundings, serves to "bring the outside in" and enhance the sense of unity with nature.

The Spa has garnered numerous awards for its eco-friendly design features, aesthetic beauty, and spa offerings, including being named by *Conde Nast Traveler* magazine in 2013 as the Number One Resort Spa in the United States.

Photo: Jim Smith Photography

The pool's wooden beams and interior are similar in feel to the skating pavilion and reflect the architectural detailing of the Main Dining Room.

Chronology

1869   Albert K. Smiley purchased from John F. Stokes approximately 300 acres and a small tavern that became Mohonk Mountain House.

1870   The House opened for its first season on June 1.

         Wallkill Valley Railroad completed to New Paltz, facilitating more direct access for arriving Mohonk guests.

         Old Stage Road built—the first in a series of new carriage roads constructed between 1870 and 1910.

         First Sky Top observation tower built; blew down after one month.

         Ice first harvested from lake for summer use; discontinued 94 years later in 1964; ice-making machines first purchased in 1965.

1870   House expanded to accommodate more guests, the first of thirteen building additions undertaken over the next thirty years.

1871   Alfred H. Smiley began actively managing Mohonk for his brother Albert.

         First paths and trails developed for guest use.

1872   Second Sky Top tower built; burned down in 1877.

1873   Telegraph office installed; discontinued in 1953.

1874   Indoor plumbing first became available for guests.

1875   Lake first stocked with fish, 2,000 smallmouth bass.

1876   Bowling "Saloon" with four alleys constructed.

         First summerhouses and bridges built at bathing beach.

1878   Third Sky Top tower built; burned down in 1909.

1879   Albert K. Smiley appointed to Board of Indian Commissioners by President Hayes.

Alfred H. Smiley left Mohonk and opened the first of two Lake Minnewaska Houses.

1880   **Wooden observation tower built on Eagle Cliff; taken down in 1973.**

1881   **Daniel Smiley became manager.**

1882   **Post office established at Mohonk.**

1883   **First Lake Mohonk Conference of Friends of the Indian convened.**

Electric call bell system (the "Annunciator") installed in 165 guest rooms, replacing speaking tubes in halls.

Livery stable built in present garden.

1885   **Mountain Rest Boarding House opened for guests, located near current Gatehouse; destroyed by fire in 1907.**

1888   **Old stable in the garden torn down and replaced by current stable for 120 horses.**

1889   **First Picnic Lodge opened for use by day visitors, later replaced by the present one in 1907.**

1890   **Stone Summerhouse completed for total cost of $193.86.**

Electric lights installed, with generating equipment housed in former Ice House.

First hydraulic elevator installed.

Small Reservoir built and new water system laid out.

First Mohonk Conference on the Negro Question convened.

1895   **Large Reservoir, later called Lily Pond, built for fire protection.**

Conference on International Arbitration convened its first meeting.

1896   **Cooperative Weather Station established at Mohonk.**

1897   **Golf "grounds" laid out (nine holes).**

1898   Garden Road (originally called Bicycle Road) built.

Weeping beech tree on Garden Road planted by founder Albert K. Smiley.

Two-story summerhouse in the garden constructed, copied from a design by Andrew Jackson Downing.

Putting green created.

First private bathrooms installed

1900   First Illumination of the Mountain for Fourth of July evening ceremony with orchestrated display of multicolored flares reflecting on boulders and cliff faces between the lake and Sky Top

Second hydraulic elevator installed.

1901   Power House completed; DC electric power generated.

1902   Long-distance telephone service inaugurated.

Bugler assigned to announce meals and entertainments, replacing ringing of bell; practice discontinued in the mid-1950s.

Fountain by East Porch constructed.

1903   First Golf Clubhouse built at Mountain Rest.

1904   Mohonk Spring House dedicated; supplied drinking water from 1870s to 1926.

1905   Greenhouse constructed.

Athletic field built.

In a Parlor talk, founder Albert K. Smiley remarked that there were currently 172 summerhouses, his brother Alfred having built the first one around 1871.

1907   Groundbreaking for the Testimonial Gateway commemorating the fiftieth wedding anniversary of founders Albert K. and Eliza Smiley.

1908   Mohonk Hose Company No. 1 founded, chartered by New York State; equipment included two horse-drawn ladder trucks that could be outfitted with sled runners for winter use.

Kleinekill Lake (Duck Pond) constructed.

1910   **Four clay tennis courts built.**

First automobile garages built at Mountain Rest, for guest cars.

Family meeting minutes indicated annual income from sale of fifty-four barrels of grease to soap companies; Mohonk's Rendering Plant operated for many decades to "recycle" fat and grease.

1912   **Daniel Smiley became proprietor upon death of founder Albert K. Smiley.**

Croquet court laid out.

1915   **Sawmill installed to cut lumber from chestnut trees killed by Asiatic blight.**

1916   **Motion pictures first shown on an outdoor screen.**

Automobiles first purchased and used at Mohonk—a Ford and two Overlands.

1917   **Motor trucks first purchased by Mohonk—Federal trucks with solid tires.**

New kind of efficient ("HRT—horizontal return tubular") steam boiler installed.

Last of the wood-burning stoves removed; radiators installed in guest rooms.

Arbitration and Indian conferences both discontinued because of World War I.

Mohonk guests, employees, and Smiley family members assisted in World War I Red Cross work to produce over 7,000 items (a dozen kinds of cloth bandages, clothing, and bedding) to be sent to France on behalf of war relief efforts.

1918   **Mohonk "Country Fair" first held, for benefit of French War Relief.**

First rental cottage built at Mountain Rest.

1920   **Mohonk's fiftieth-anniversary ceremony held.**

Mohonk School founded by Mabel C. Smiley as a private boarding school for boys—located at Mohonk Mountain House until 1958.

Lake first stocked with trout; *The Mohonk Bulletin* notes that 20,000 food fish were introduced in the lake, with artificial food being supplied in numerous sunken wire cylinders

Farm ledger showed 1,024 pigs being raised at Mohonk's pig farm; pig farm operation discontinued in the 1950s after 80 years, with poultry and sheep operations having been phased out several decades earlier.

1923   **Fourth tower on Sky Top, constructed from stone quarried on the site, completed as a memorial to founder Albert K. Smiley.**

Inventory of Mohonk buildings showed a total of 199 structures (188 insured), including buildings in the resort complex, at Mountain Rest, on the farms, and tenant houses.

Forest fire observers stationed at Sky Top employed by New York State Conservation Department.

1925   **Golf course expanded to eighteen holes; back nine holes aptly called "Hillside," with one hole called "Down" and another called "Way Down."**

1926   **Sky Top Reservoir completed as part of the fire protection system.**

Mossy Brook Spring water first pumped up from the foot of the mountain to the House.

1930   **Smiley Brothers Partnership formed, with second-generation brothers Albert K. Smiley and Francis G. Smiley taking over proprietorship following death of Daniel Smiley.**

1931   **First automatic sprinklers installed for fire protection.**

1933   **Power plant switched to burning substantial amounts of cordwood instead of coal because of the Great Depression.**

Part of Mountain House first kept open for guests during the winter.

1934   **Ice skating on the lake became available for guests.**

1935   First rock climbing activity on Trapps Cliffs, south of Mountain House.

"Garden Lovers' Holiday" offered, first of many "theme programs" to follow.

1940   **Lawn bowling green created.**

Mohonk's woodland put under management of full-time forester.

1941   **Labor for wood-chopping totaled 4,686 "man days" for the year to heat the Mountain House with wood.**

Fire engine acquired for Mohonk Hose Company No. 1.

1948   **First of three shuffleboard courts built.**

1951   **Milk pasteurization plant installed; discontinued in 1965 when Mohonk Farms Dairy operation terminated.**

1953   **Smiley Brothers Partnership expanded to include third-generation family members —brothers Daniel Smiley, Jr. and Albert K. Smiley, Jr., and cousin Gerow Smiley.**

1955   **First use of fuel oil in power plant boilers instead of coal and cordwood.**

1958   **First AC electric power used at Mohonk, supplied by Central Hudson Gas and Electric Corporation.**

1960   **Bowling alley reconstructed as a meeting hall named Council House to attract more conference business.**

1963   **The Mohonk Trust (now the Mohonk Preserve) founded by Smiley family members and Mohonk friends as a not-for-profit land trust, with goals related to the family's long-held land stewardship concerns and world social issues.**

The golf course hole called "Down" adapted during winter season as a downhill ski slope with four rope tows; golf course reverted to nine holes in 1968.

1965   **Granary building moved from deer paddock to present location above bathing beach and reconfigured for seasonal meal service.**

1966   **First conveyance of Mohonk land to The Mohonk Trust (now the Mohonk Preserve) for preservation as open space.**

1968   Present electric elevators installed, replacing former hydraulic model known as "Big Elevator."

1969   Mohonk's centennial year celebrated with special events; time capsule buried by the rock on the putting green.

Smiley Brothers Partnership incorporated, becoming Smiley Brothers, Inc., with business operating under a board of directors; officers elected—third-generation Daniel Smiley, Jr. as chairman, brother Albert K. Smiley as president, and cousin Benjamin H. Matteson as executive vice president.

1970   First organized ski touring, with equipment rental and lessons provided.

1972   Barn Museum opened.

Forest fire observers at Sky Top replaced by air surveillance.

1973   Lake Mohonk Mountain House complex recognized as a place of architectural and historical significance and listed on National Register of Historic Places by United States Department of the Interior.

1977   New Greenhouse constructed.

Riding ring built at site of former Ice House.

"Mystery Weekend" program created, becoming immensely popular and subsequently imitated in numerous venues elsewhere.

Two all-weather tennis courts constructed.

1979   Telephones installed in all guest rooms.

Two platform tennis courts constructed.

1980   Mohonk Consultations established by Albert K. Smiley, Jr. as a not-for-profit organization carrying on Smiley family tradition of bringing people together to discuss the interrelationships of all life on Earth, with emphasis on the sustainable use of the Earth's resources.

1982   First computer installed, for use in the Reservations and Front Desk accounting departments.

1983   First fitness center opened, in basement of Mountain House.

Summerhouse silhouette became Mohonk's official logo, registered with the U.S. Patent and Trademark Office.

1985   Bernard L. Gavin appointed chief executive officer of Smiley Brothers, Inc.

1986   Mohonk Mountain House, with its surrounding 7,800 acres of land (including acreage transferred to Mohonk Preserve) designated as a National Historic Landmark by United States Department of the Interior.

1988   Donald D. Woodworth became president of Mohonk Mountain House.

1989   Mohonk Mountain House registered with Historic Hotels of America by National Trust for Historic Preservation.

Festival of the Arts founded by Patricia Smiley Guralnik and her husband Robert Guralnik.

1990   Fourth-generation Albert K. Smiley elected president and CEO of Smiley Brothers, Inc.

Conference House constructed.

1992   First air-conditioning installed in the Mountain House (East Dining Room).

New, centralized composting system implemented by Gerow Smiley; from Mohonk's first years composting included recycling garbage, manure, plant trimmings, and wood ashes for use on farm fields and gardens.

1994   Mohonk Mountain House and the Smiley family received award from United Nations Environment Programme recognizing 125 years of environmental stewardship and dedicated leadership.

1998   "Mohonk Kids' Club" launched, offering expanded children's activities.

1999   Mohonk Hose Company No. 1 resurrected, with employee residents as volunteer fire fighters; new firehouse constructed; used fire engine purchased.

Fourth of July fireworks used again for the first time in 100 years, as the multicolored flares previously used became unavailable.

About the Author

Larry E. Burgess received his B.A. in history from the University of Redlands and his M.A. and Ph.D. in history from the Claremont Graduate University.

Dr. Burgess served as founding Archivist and Head of Special Collections of A.K. Smiley Public Library from 1972 to 1985, and as Director of the library from 1986 to 2012. Since retirement in 2012, he now serves as Director Emeritus for the A.K. Smiley Public Library and gives many programs a year on a variety of subjects relating to the history of Southern California, the West, and Lincoln and the Civil War.

Burgess has served on many regional boards and commissions. He is vice chair of the Board of the University of Redlands, and was vice chair of the California Historic Preservation Commission (1982–84). He chaired the City of Redlands U.S. Bicentennial Committee (1976), the University of Redlands 75th Anniversary Committee (1981–82), and the City of Redlands Centennial celebration (1988). He was president of the Zamorano Club of Los Angeles, a rare book association, and presently is editor of its quarterly publication *Hoja Violante*. He is a past president of the Historical Society of Southern California, and is on the advisory board of the Abraham Lincoln Bicentennial Commission.

Additionally, Burgess was an adjunct professor in the graduate department of history at the University of California, Riverside and University of Redlands.

Burgess is the author of many books including: introductory summary, "What is a Woman Worth?", *The Woman's National Indian Association: A History* (2015), edited by Valerie Mathes; *Faithfully & Liberally Sustained: Philanthropy in Redlands* (2010), co-authored with Nathan D. Gonzales; *Redlands in Transition* (2008), coauthored with Nathan D. Gonzales; *With Unbounded Confidence, A Centennial History of the University of Redlands* (2006); *Images of America: Redlands* (2004), coauthored with Nathan D. Gonzales; *The Smileys: A Biography* (1969, 1993); *Mohonk: It's People and Spirit* (1982, 1993); *Daniel Smiley of Mohonk: A Naturalist's Life* (1996); *The Hunt for Willie Boy* (1994), coauthored with James A. Sandos and named Outstanding Book on the subject of human rights in North America by the Gustavus Myers Center For The Study of Human Rights (1995); and *Willie Boy in Two Worlds: An Episode in Indian-White Relations*, coauthored with James A. Sandos in *True Stories from the American Past: Since 1865*, edited by William Graebner (2002).

Dr. Burgess resides with his wife Charlotte, Vice President for External Affairs & Dean Emerita at the University of Redlands, in their 1890 Victorian grove house in Redlands.

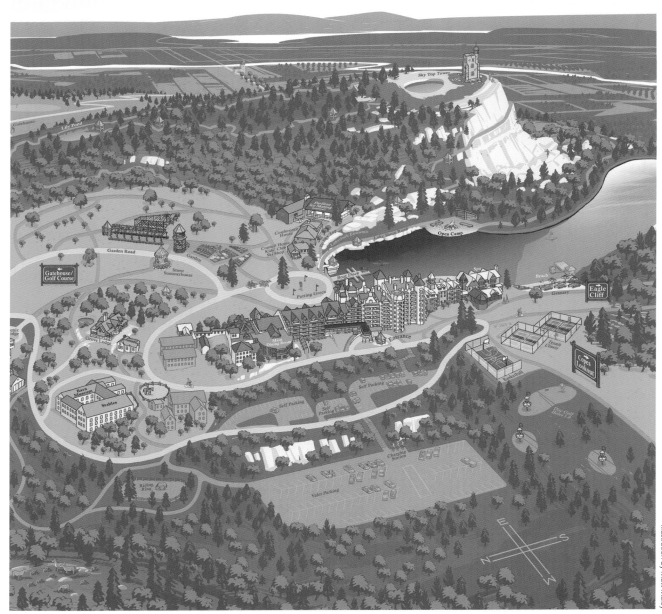

Illustration by Matt Maley